T0323582

Cambridge Elements ≡

Elements in the Philosophy of Physics
edited by
James Owen Weatherall
University of California, Irvine

GAUGE THEORY AND THE GEOMETRIZATION OF PHYSICS

Henrique De Andrade Gomes
University of Oxford

Shaftesbury Road, Cambridge CB2 8EA, United Kingdom

One Liberty Plaza, 20th Floor, New York, NY 10006, USA

477 Williamstown Road, Port Melbourne, VIC 3207, Australia

314–321, 3rd Floor, Plot 3, Splendor Forum, Jasola District Centre,
New Delhi – 110025, India

103 Penang Road, #05–06/07, Visioncrest Commercial, Singapore 238467

Cambridge University Press is part of Cambridge University Press & Assessment,
a department of the University of Cambridge.

We share the University's mission to contribute to society through the pursuit of
education, learning and research at the highest international levels of excellence.

www.cambridge.org
Information on this title: www.cambridge.org/9781009548113

DOI: 10.1017/9781009029308

© Henrique De Andrade Gomes 2025

When citing this work, please include a reference to the DOI 10.1017/9781009029308

First published 2025

A catalogue record for this publication is available from the British Library

ISBN 978-1-009-54811-3 Hardback
ISBN 978-1-009-01408-3 Paperback
ISSN 2632-413X (online)
ISSN 2632-4121 (print)

Gauge Theory and the Geometrization of Physics

Elements in the Philosophy of Physics

DOI: 10.1017/9781009029308
First published online: January 2025

Henrique De Andrade Gomes
University of Oxford

Author for correspondence: Henrique De Andrade Gomes,
gomes.ha@gmail.com

Abstract: This Element is broadly about the geometrization of physics, but mostly it is about gauge theories. Gauge theories lie at the heart of modern physics: in particular, they constitute the Standard Model of particle physics. At its simplest, the idea of gauge is that nature is best described using a descriptively redundant language; the different descriptions are said to be related by a gauge symmetry. The overarching question this Element aims to answer is: why is descriptive redundancy fruitful for physics? I will provide three interrelated answers to the question: "Why gauge theory?" that is: why introduce redundancies in our models of nature in the first place? The first is pragmatic, or methodological; the second is based on geometrical considerations, and the third is broadly relational.

Keywords: Gauge theory, symmetry, fiber bundles, affine geometry, Noether's theorems

ISBNs: 9781009548113 (HB), 9781009014083 (PB), 9781009029308 (OC)
ISSNs: 2632-413X (online), 2632-4121 (print)

Contents

1 Introduction

1.1 Gauge Theories

Gauge theories lie at the heart of modern physics: in particular, they constitute the Standard Model of particle physics. But they have so far received far less philosophical analysis than the other revolutions of twentieth-century physics, namely, relativity and quantum mechanics. This is unfortunate, since they raise many philosophical questions.

For example: at its simplest, the idea of gauge is that nature is best described using a descriptively redundant language. This idea is tied to important topics in philosophy: Putnam's permutation argument, structural scientific realism, Fregean sense and reference, to mention just a few. But in this context, the idea also prompts a conceptual puzzle: how can mere redundancy be scientifically fruitful and explanatory? Here, we will focus on this last puzzle, and try to give some answers. But first, we need to know what gauge theory is in more detail.

The first thing to say is that gauge theory is about symmetries. As a first approximation, we can think of a symmetry of a physical theory as a map (function) on the physical states that the theory attributes to the system it describes. The important property of this map is that it preserves the values of a salient, usually large, set of physical quantities of the system. Of course, this broad idea is made precise in various different ways: for example as a map on the space of states, or on the set of quantities; and as a map that must respect the system's dynamics, for example, by mapping solutions to solutions or even by preserving the value of the Lagrangian.

But what makes a symmetry "gauge"? In the dictionary, "to gauge" means "to estimate or measure." Historically, the relation to this dictionary meaning comes from Weyl (1929), who introduced gauge fields in an attempt to understand electromagnetism as a measure of length-change along a curve in spacetime (I will give a brief historical timeline in Section 1.3). But that original meaning bears little resemblance to how "gauge" is understood today.

Today, we say *gauge theory* is a theory that has local symmetries: symmetries whose action on the local state of a system over a given spacetime region does not determine its action on the state over any nonoverlapping region.

The states with which gauge theories are concerned are described by fields over spacetime: we have a space of determinables over each spacetime point, and fixing a particular state or value of a field fixes a determinate value over each spacetime point. This is very much like the description of states of general relativity, which are described by metric and matter tensors. So what are the possible values of the states of gauge theory? In our most current understanding of particle physics – given by what's called "the Standard Model," developed in the and 1960s and 1970s – there are many fields: one for each particle type. So we have an electron field, a photon field, a gluon field, a quark field, a Higgs field, and so on. Gauge theory parts ways from general relativity in that the value space of these fields is not "soldered" onto spacetime. It has a rich structure that is not just supervenient on the properties of space and time.

And as to gauge symmetries, they are more than mere solution-preserving maps on the space of solutions of the theory: they are characterized independently of the states or quantities on which they act, forming a group whose elements can also be seen as points of a smooth manifold. In short: gauge symmetries are described by *Lie groups*. For illustration, the symmetry group of the Standard Model is called $SU(3) \times SU(2) \times U(1)$, and we will have more to say about it in Section 4. The action of a gauge group on each spacetime point severely constrains, or partially determines, the properties of the particles of the Standard Model, who must vary in a prescribed manner under the action of this group.

Summing up this quick introduction of gauge symmetries, they are usually understood as: (i) leaving points of spacetime invariant, and (ii) not affecting the physical states of the system.

But both (i) and (ii) are somewhat flexible. Many physicists call the symmetries of general relativity "gauge", and these don't satisfy (i); and as to (ii), though physicists will agree that a gauge transformation has the connotation of being empirically undetectable, they are less concerned about whether symmetry-related states are metaphysically identical.

In contrast, for philosophers, faced with a symmetry, the obvious question is: do the two states thus related represent the same physical state of affairs? Of course, this was the very question at the center of Newton's dispute with Leibniz, encapsulated in the Leibniz-Clarke Correspondence. It has resonated down the centuries, and rightly so: it lies at the center of natural philosophy. For it raises a cluster of good logico-philosophical questions about the identity of objects (both bodies, and spatial points and spacetime points), and about possibility: some of them linked, for example, whether some version of the principle of the identity of indiscernibles is true.

I will, of course, not be able to rehash these questions here; this is a short introduction! In fact, I won't be able to comprehensively review any of these topics even in the narrow case of gauge theory. So, like most politicians, when faced with a tough question I will answer a different, easier one (and hope the audience doesn't notice). I will approach the many questions about gauge symmetry and equivalence only obliquely, by drawing parallels between the case of bona-fide gauge theories and general relativity; the foremost example of a spacetime theory with symmetries. The hope is to show that, to the extent that one can draw certain kinds of conclusions – about contentious topics such as locality and physical equivalence – in the case of general relativity, there is very good reason to believe that these conclusions also apply to gauge theories.

General relativity is a thoroughly "geometricised" theory, and so it pays to understand gauge theory also through geometry. The geometrical theory that deals with symmetry groups acting at each spacetime point is called *the theory of fiber bundles*. In this formalism, the mathematical object determining how the photon, the gluons, or, more generally, how internal states of all particles, evolve is called *the gauge potential*.

Historically, gauge theory was not introduced geometrically. It was a tool used to simplify the field equations of electromagnetism using the gauge potential, and the inherent ambiguity in its representation – the origin of gauge freedom – was considered an indication that the potential lacked physical meaning. The geometrization of this theory and its generalizations was one the most formidable examples of an unintentional convergence between physics and mathematics. As C.N. Yang (1983, p. 567) recollects:

> The Maxwell equations and the principles of quantum mechanics led to the idea of gauge invariance. Attempts to generalize this idea, motivated by physical concepts of phases, symmetries, and conservation laws, led to the theory of non-Abelian gauge fields. That non-Abelian gauge fields are conceptually identical to ideas in the beautiful theory of bundles, developed by mathematicians without reference to the physical world, left me astounded. In 1975, I discussed my considerations with Chern and said, "This is both exciting and perplexing, as you mathematicians invented these concepts out of nothing." Immediately, he protested, "No, no. These concepts were not dreamed up. They were natural and real."

And it is indeed true that Yang and Mills were exclusively seeking a generalization of Maxwell's equations, with no knowledge of a geometric interpretation via bundles (an interpretation that we aim to delve into). Their quest was more than justified on purely physical grounds: the theory of quantum electrodynamics is one of the most successful in the history of physics. The goal of physics (or that of a significant portion of physicists) was then (and perhaps still is) to place all particles on the same footing as the photon.

1.2 Roadmap for This Element

First, I should be clear about my intentions. I don't want to merely repeat or summarize what is easily found in the literature. I want to advertise my own, sometimes novel, understanding of gauge theory. I will try to be clear about what is orthodoxy and what is not; *the unorthodox will be marked with a #*. Likewise, some sections will go slow, and be appropriate for a beginning graduate student, covering more standard material; others will require more mathematical background, and be more suitable for the professional researcher: *the more advanced will be marked with a* ∗.

After setting so many topics aside, and being forthright about my intentions, let me tell you what you *will* find in this Element.

It is often said that it is not the business of physics, and science more generally, to ask "why" things happen the way that they do; its purview is only to ask "how." This motto may rightly apply to some teleological ideas which have been long abandoned in physics. But nowadays, whenever a new formalism is introduced, physicists – and philosophers of physics even more so – want to understand *why* it is necessary. If we are going to postulate a rich internal structure to our theories and, perhaps more surprisingly, transformations of our models that correspond to no empirical difference (as per (ii) previously), we better have good reason to do so.

In my view, there are many answers to the "why" question. Unfortunately, I only have space to focus on two of them, which will be given in Sections 2 and 4; and I will skim a third reason in Section 5. The first is pragmatic, the second is geometrical, and the third is relational. All three are compatible, and indeed complementary.[1]

In Section 2 I will discuss a methodological reason to introduce more degrees of freedom than are to be counted as physically distinguishing. We will see that gauge redundancy is useful for constructing new theories for a very specific reason, related to Noether's famous theorems. The purpose of this section is to provide a good practical reason to introduce gauge, or redundant, degrees of freedom, so it will assume certain properties of gauge fields, leaving their conceptual and mathematical treatment to the next section.

Section 3 will thus present the modern mathematical view of gauge theory and give a conceptual appraisal of the variables involved. Here I will introduce the theory of fiber bundles: the appropriate mathematical formalism to talk about "internal (or value) spaces" over spacetime. (Although there are several good textbooks with the mathematical machinery expounded in this section, I think none cover the subset that I think is most important for the conceptually minded physicist or philosopher; and none strike quite the balance between rigor and simplicity that I am aiming for.) The overarching conceptual theme of this section is that the modern mathematical view involves understanding gauge symmetries geometrically, as more like spacetime symmetries.

---

[1] And none of them coincide with the historical origin of gauge symmetry. The historical reasons for the introduction of the full power of modern gauge theory are many and intricate: the success of QED and the deluge of data from experimental particle physics cried out for organizing principles, and the most successful ones employed symmetries. But I won't enter this tangled part of history.

In Section 4 this analogy will be fully expanded and expounded. Here, using the machinery of Section 3, I give a very brief introduction of the Standard Model. I will argue that, as far as physics is concerned, the local symmetries of gauge theory are very closely analogous to the local Lorentz symmetry of spacetime. In this analogy, neither kind of symmetry is fundamental, both arise as sets of transformations that preserve a local geometric structure – of an internal vector space in the case of gauge theory and of the metric of spacetime in general relativity, respectively.

It would be impossible to write an introduction to gauge theory without mentioning the Aharonov–Bohm effect in electromagnetism – a philosopher's favorite! The effect is important because it supposedly captures a phenomenon that cannot be described using only local, gauge invariant quantities. So I will finish this Element by setting the Aharonov–Bohm effect firmly within the geometric formalism, and discussing what is the appropriate notion of non-locality that the Aharonov–Bohm effect evinces. But more importantly, I will use the effect to discuss nonlocality and nonseparability, and their relationship to gauge theory.

Now I will end this introduction with a brief historical timeline, recounting the most important steps in the development of gauge theories, in both physics and mathematics. An excellent source for this material is O'Raifertaigh (1997).

1.3 Historical Timeline

1.3.1 In Physics

- 1918–19: Weyl's "unified theory"/infinitesimal geometry introduces gauge (Eichung) rescaling symmetry.
- 1929: Weyl introduces the gauge principle for the Abelian group U(1) in quantum mechanics, in order to "explain" Maxwell's theory of electromagnetism.
- 1954: Yang & Mills, and Shaw, produce the first non-Abelian gauge theory for the group SU(2) (as an attempt to describe the strong interaction between proton/neutron as a doublet).
- 1954–55: Independently, R. Utiyama develops the framework of gauge theory for any Lie group G. He shows that general relativity is, in a certain sense, a gauge theory of the local Lorentz group $G = SO(1, 3)$.
- 1960s–70s: By a series of rapid developments, the Standard Model of particle theory arises (electroweak unification by Glashow in 1961; spontaneous symmetry breaking (SSB) mechanism by Englert-Brout-Higgs in 1964, Quarks by Gell-Mann and Zweig in 1964, electroweak theory with SSB by Weinberg and Salam in 1967, renormalizability by 't Hooft 1971; asymptotic

freedom by Politzer (and Gross and Wilczek) in 1973, etc.). Particle physics is described as a gauge field theory of with gauge group $G = U(1) \times SU(2) \times SU(3)$.

1.3.2 In Mathematics

- 1916–17: Theory of connections on manifolds by Levi-Civita, Schouten.
- 1918–19: Weyl's infinitesimal geometry falls within this current of ideas.
- 1920s: Cartan's "espaces generalisés," a vast synthesis of (pseudo-) Riemannian and Klein geometries.
- 1930s: Whitney's first definition of fibered spaces, or fiber bundles: spaces with "structured points".
- 1950s–60s: Mature theory of connections on fiber bundles (Ehresmann, 1950; Steenrod, 1951; Kobayashi, 1957)

The two strands finally converged in the mid-1970s. In 1975, T. T. Wu and C.N. Yang published a paper about the physicist's electromagnetic field theory and its relationship to the mathematician's fiber bundle theory (Wu & Yang, 1975). To clarify the deep – and precise – relation between these two strands, they constructed a dictionary. In 1976 Isadore Singer visited Stony Brook and Yang gave him a copy of the Wu-Yang preprint, which Singer took to Oxford. There, Michael Atiyah and other mathematicians studied the paper and began to work on gauge fields and related topics, leading to a period of close collaboration between mathematicians and physicists. Figure 1 is a table taken from a paper in this period.

Wu & Yang Dictionary, 1975

Gauge field terminology	Bundle terminology
gauge (or global gauge)	principal coordinate bundle
gauge type	principal fibre bundle
gauge potential b_μ^k	connection on a principal fibre bundle
S_{ba}	transition function
phase factor Φ_{QP}	parallel displacement
field strength $f_{\mu\nu}^k$	curvature
source[1] J_μ^k	?[2]
electromagnetism	connection in a $U_1(1)$ bundle
isotopic spin gauge field	connection in a SU_2 bundle
Dirac's monopole quantization	classification of $U_1(1)$ bundle according to first Chern class
electromagnetism without monopole	connection on a trivial $U_1(1)$ bundle
electromagnetism with monopole	connection to a nontrivial $U_1(1)$ bundle

Figure 1 The Wu-Yang Dictionary, as described by Isadore Singer, in an article about Weyl in Wells (1988).

2 Why Gauge? A Noether, Methodological Reason

All interpretations of modern gauge theories adopt two core assumptions at their foundation. The first is that gauge symmetry arises when there are more variables in a theory than there are physical degrees of freedom. Hence the well-known soubriquets: gauge is "descriptive redundancy," "surplus structure," and "descriptive fluff." Correspondingly, considerable effort has been devoted to techniques for eliminating gauge redundancy in order to appropriately interpret gauge theories.[2] The second assumption is that a theory with gauge symmetry constitutes the gold standard of a modern physical theory: witness the gauge symmetry invoked in the Standard Model. This leads to a remarkable *puzzle of gauge symmetry:* if interpreting gauge symmetry requires eliminating it, then why is gauge symmetry so ubiquitous?

The purpose of this section is to articulate one answer to this question: namely, that gauge symmetry provides a path to building appropriate dynamical theories – and that this rationale invokes the two theorems of Emmy Noether (1918).[3] Noether's first and better-known theorem (commonly called simply *Noether's theorem*) implies that global (or what we will call *rigid*) symmetries of a classical Lagrangian field theory – that is, symmetries in which the redundancy is specified in exactly the same way at all spacetime points – correspond to charges that are conserved over time, such as energy and angular momentum. For example, the conservation of an electron's charge can be viewed as arising from the (redundant) global phases of the electron's wavefunction. But we will be equally concerned with Noether's second theorem, which is about local, or what I will also call *malleable*) gauge symmetries – meaning that the specified redundancy varies between spacetime points. Although these theorems' physical significance is, of course, already well recognized, including in the philosophical literature (Brading & Brown, 2000, 2003), in this section I will urge that these two theorems give us a further answer to the puzzle, "why gauge?"

To get the gist of the argument to come, let us take the example of the electron field. As we know, the charges carried by electrons are sources for electromagnetic fields. And we take the interaction between the electric charges to be mediated by the electromagnetic field; and we measure the electromagnetic field by its effect on electric charges. But just like spacetime has its own dynamics in general relativity, electromagnetic fields have their own

---

[2] Cf. Earman (2002, 2003, 2004), Healey (2007), and Rosenstock & Weatherall (2016, 2018).

[3] For details on the historical development of Noether's theorems see Kosmann-Schwarzbach (2011). For a modern statement of the first and second theorems, cf. Olver (1986), Theorems 5.58 (p. 334) and 5.66 (p. 343) respectively.

dynamics, even in the absence of charges: there are nontrivial solutions of the Maxwell equations even in vacuum; for example, an electromagnetic plane wave.

Thus suppose that we are canvassing the possibilities for the dynamical laws of a field that is sourced by a charge – call it the force field – and that we want to ensure that charge was conserved. Suppose further that for each possible dynamical law we should be able to infer the quantity of charge in a sufficiently small region of space via the behavior of the force field surrounding this region, as I described previously. But certain dynamics of the force field would not permit this kind of inference: think of field lines emanating from a given region of space that suddenly vanish, or diminish in density. Charges might be conserved, but in this case we could never infer the charge contained in a region by its effect on other charges. So, if charges are to interact via the force field and are to be conserved, it is natural to impose a consistency constraint on the dynamics of the force fields. Simply put: conservation of material charges requires compatible dynamics of the force fields. This constraint applies to all interactions and all charges of the Standard Model of particle physics and general relativity. Indeed, such constraints will need to be imposed even for those conserved charges and associated interactions that we have not yet come across in our theorizing.

And such constraints are not methodologically idle. Indeed they have often guided the formulation of our theories: before gauge theory, scientists such as Einstein and Maxwell proposed early versions of the dynamics for the fields of their respective theories that did *not* satisfy these constraints, and both of them had many a headache for that reason. It was precisely this kind of consistency that eventually led them to postulate the final form of their equations.[4]

One of the main merits of gauge theories is that they allow us to "cut out the middle man" that is this method of trial and error. How do they do this?

In gauge theories, the symmetries are local – their action on one space-time region is independent of their action elsewhere. Noether's *second* theorem applies to this kind of symmetry, but, unlike her first theorem, which applies to global, or rigid symmetries, it gives no straightforward conservation law; it only implies that the equations of motion are not all independent from each

---

[4] In Maxwell's case, he found the Biot-Savart law from ensuring conservation of charge. And Einstein had several attempts before finally settling on his now well-known field equations. In his case, it was ensuring that the purely geometric side of his equations respected the same conservation law as the side including matter.

other. In other words, the theorem says that there are fewer independent equations of motion than there are degrees of freedom for it. Thus the original degrees of freedom are *constrained*: it is only a constrained subset of the original degrees of freedom at some initial time that is uniquely, deterministically, propagated to the future; (see e.g. Brading & Brown (2003) for a conceptual overview).

Since the set of local symmetries contains the global symmetries, which are responsible for charge conservation via Noether's first theorem, when we extend global to local symmetries, there should emerge a relationship between charge conservation according to Noether's first theorem and the constraints that arise via Noether's second theorem. And surely enough, a relationship does emerge. The amazing, even if not entirely surprising, fact about this relationship is that it is precisely the one required for consistency between charge conservation and the dynamics of the interacting field.

This answer to the question of "why gauge" is an instance of the much more general role for gauge, which I have sketched previously, and which has not been at all discussed in the philosophical literature: gauge symmetry supports theory construction. Although some philosophers like Brading and Brown (2003) have pointed out the role of gauge symmetry in theory construction, a more specific answer to the puzzle of gauge symmetry that I will advocate here is that it constrains the coupling of charges to forces. This construal of the gauge argument is, to an extent idiosyncratic. But, as experts will be quick to note: the usual gauge argument in its common textbook form is fraught with difficulties.

Here is the roadmap for the remainder of this section. In Section 2.1 I will rehearse the usual gauge argument and its woes. In Section 2.2, I will present the much more general gauge argument sketched previously, which I will call the *Noether gauge argument*, in the context of classical Lagrangian field theory. The key to understanding this argument is the combined use of *both* Noether's first *and* second theorems.

2.1 The Gauge Argument and Its Critics

The textbook gauge argument or gauge principle uses gauge invariance to motivate a quantum theory of electromagnetism. We begin Section 2.1.1 with a brief presentation of this argument as it is usually presented. Classic textbook statements can be found in Schutz (1980, §6.14), Göckeler & Schücker (1989, §4.2), and Ryder (1996, §3.3), among many other places. Then in Section 2.1.2 we assess it. The argument has been discussed in the form herein by philosophers as well, such as Teller (1997, 2000), Brown (1999), Martin (2002), and Wallace (2009, §2). To the end of Section 2, I will take a very pragmatic approach: I will leave a more conceptual introduction to the variables of gauge theory to Section 3.

2.1.1 Beware: Dubious Arguments Ahead

We begin by describing a quantum system with the Hilbert space $L^2(\mathbb{R}^3)$ of wavefunctions, recalling that a unique pure quantum state is represented not by vector, but by a "rays" of vectors related by a complex unit. This implies that the transformation $\psi(\vec{x}) \mapsto e^{i\theta}\psi(\vec{x})$ for some $\theta \in \mathbb{R}$, referred to as a "global phase" transformation, acts identically on rays, and is in this sense an invariance of the quantum system.[5] This invariance is incorporated in the specification of the dynamics of the system, either via the Hamiltonian or the action, since either contains only real valued functions such as $|\psi|^2$ and $\partial_i\psi\partial_i\bar{\psi}$.

But now, the story goes, suppose we replace this global phase with a "local phase" transformation $\psi(\vec{x}) \mapsto e^{i\phi(\vec{x})}\psi(\vec{x})$, in which the constant θ is replaced with a function $\phi : \mathbb{R}^3 \to \mathbb{R}$, or indeed with a smooth one-parameter family of such functions $\phi_t(\vec{x})$ for each $t \in \mathbb{R}$; or, adopting the covariant notation in which $x = (t,\vec{x})$, we write as $\phi(x)$. This transformation is "local" in the sense that its values vary smoothly across space and time.

The corresponding Hilbert space map $R_\phi : \psi \mapsto e^{i\phi}\psi$ does not act identically on rays. As to the dynamics, whereas $|\psi|^2$ would remain invariant under such a transformation, that would not be the case for terms involving derivatives, such as $\partial_i\psi\partial_i\bar{\psi}$, which under such a transformation acquires terms depending on $\partial_i\phi$ such as $(\partial_i\phi)^2\psi\bar{\psi}$.

However, one might still wish to postulate that this transformation has no "physical effect" on the system, or is "gauge." Various motivations for this step are given in the textbooks, often with vague references to general covariance of the kind found in general relativity. But to mimic the standard presentation, we will simply press forward, referring to $R_\phi : \psi \mapsto e^{i\phi}\psi$ as a *local* or *malleable gauge transformation*.

---

[5] Here $e^{i\phi} = e^{i\phi+2\pi}$, and the symmetry group in question is called $U(1) := \{e^{i\theta}, \theta \in \mathbb{R}\}$. It is a group G since for any $g, h, k \in G$ it satisfies the axioms: (1) $(g \cdot h) \cdot k = g \cdot (h \cdot k)$; (2) $g \cdot \text{Id} = g$; and (3) $g \cdot g^{-1} = \text{Id}$, where "$\cdot$" is the group action, and Id is the group identity. In the case of $U(1)$, the action is just multiplication: $e^{i\theta_1}e^{i\theta_2} = e^{i\theta_1+\theta_2}$, the inverse is just the multiplicative inverse: $(e^{i\theta})^{-1} = e^{-i\theta}$, and the identity is just the multiplicative identity, the number 1. Note also that $U(1)$ has the local smooth structure of $\mathbb{R}$: in fact, it forms a smooth manifold which is just the circle, whose action can be understood as rotations in the complex plane (which is why we call it R_ϕ). This is our first example of a Lie group: we will encounter others along this Element, but we will no longer stop to demonstrate that they satisfy the definitions as we did here.

With respect to the dynamics, we still need to say something about the non-invariant terms involving derivatives. The big move of the gauge argument is to first introduce a vector $A = (A_1, A_2, A_3)$ and a scalar V, which are assumed to behave under the gauge transformation as,

$$A \mapsto A + \nabla \phi_t, \qquad\qquad V \mapsto V - \frac{d\phi_t}{dt}. \qquad\qquad (2.1.1)$$

To restore invariance of the dynamics under gauge transformations, and with an eye toward a modern gauge theory formulated as a vector bundle with a derivative operator, writing $\partial_\mu := (\frac{d}{dt}, \nabla)$ and $A_\mu = (V, A)$, one finds that one can restore gauge-invariance by replacing ∂_μ with,

$$D_\mu := \partial_\mu + iA_\mu = (\frac{d}{dt} + iV, \nabla + iA) = (D_t, D). \qquad\qquad (2.1.2)$$

This is commonly referred to as a "covariant derivative," and it has the form of the familiar gauge freedom of the electromagnetic four-potential. That is, if we call $A_0 := V$, these transformations leave invariant the following tensor:

$$F_{\mu\nu} = \partial_\mu A_\nu - \partial_\mu A_\nu, \qquad\qquad (2.1.3)$$

where the electric and magnetic field are recovered in a given coordinate system as $E_i = F_{0i}$ and $B^i = \epsilon^{ijk} F_{jk}$, where x^0 are the time coordinates, i, j, k are spatial indices, and ϵ^{ijk} is the totally anti-symmetric tensor in space. In short, it appears as if minimal electromagnetic coupling has been derived out of nothing: or at least, from an assumption of gauge invariance.

2.1.2 Criticisms of the Gauge Argument

That is how the story is usually presented. I agree: it is far from water-tight. The argument begins with a system with a global symmetry, gratuitously generalizes it to a local symmetry – which, to emphasize, was not required for mathematical consistency or for empirical adequacy – and then, in order to fix the ensuing noninvariance of the governing equations, proceeds to conjecture a new force of nature, which, so far, has no reason to be dynamical at all. Ultimately, the argument gives us no reason to think of the field A_μ as being related to Maxwell's equation. To put it uncharitably: the argument fixes a problem that didn't exist by conjecturing a redundant field, and then turns this game around, claiming to come out successfully by "retrodicting" the existence of electromagnetism. More charitably: the gauge argument suffers from at least three categories of concerns. I will set out each of these three concerns here and in Section 2.2 present an alternative *Noether gauge argument* that answers them entirely.

The first category of concerns is the gauge argument's claim to have derived a dynamics that is specifically electromagnetic in nature. Although a formal set of operators $A_\mu = (V, A)$ have been included in the dynamics, no evidence is given that these operators take the form required for any *specific* electromagnetic potential, or that the coupling to A_μ will be proportional to a particle's charge e, or even that A_μ is nonzero. And if they could be shown to be nonzero, then as Wallace (2009, p. 210) rightly asks: "how do neutral particles fit into the argument?" A minimally coupled dynamics does not apply to neutral particles, and yet since the gauge argument never mentioned or assumed anything about charge, it presumably is intended to apply to them.

A second category of problems arises out of the free-wheeling argumentative style of the gauge argument. For example, it is not a strict deductive derivation of either the electromagnetic potential or the dynamics. At best, the gauge argument appears to show that one *can* adopt a minimally coupled Hamiltonian in order to assure gauge invariance. But this does not ensure that one *must* do so: the door appears to be left open for other dynamics to be gauge invariant, but without taking the minimally coupled form that the gauge argument advocates. As Martin (2002, p. S230) writes: "The most I think we can safely say is that the form of the dynamics characteristic of successful physical (gauge) theories is *suggested* through running the gauge argument."

Another example of free-wheeling argumentation is in the motivation for requiring the local gauge transformations $R_\phi : \psi \mapsto e^{i\phi(x)}\psi$ to be symmetries. Sometimes a preference for this transformation over global phase transformations is dubiously motivated by a desire to avoid superluminal signaling.[6] In other cases it is motivated by the coordinate invariance of a spatial coordinate system. But as Wallace (2009, p. 210) points out, no reason is given as to why we do not similarly consider local transformations of configuration space, momentum space, or any other space, to be symmetries. Nor is there any clear reason why the $U(1)$ symmetry of electromagnetism is chosen as the global symmetry motivating the move to the local symmetry, as opposed (say) the $SU(3)$ symmetry of the strong nuclear force.

Regarding the generalization of the gauge argument to other global symmetry groups beyond electromagnetism, I wholeheartedly agree with Wallace: one should expect, and indeed I will argue in Section 2.2, that an appropriate generalization of the gauge argument can also be applied to these more general gauge groups.

---

[6] For example, Ryder (1996, p. 93) writes: "when we perform a rotation in the internal space of ϕ at one point, through an angle Λ, we must perform the same rotation at all other points at the same time. If we take this physical interpretation seriously, we see that it is impossible to fulfil, since it contradicts the letter and spirit of relativity, according to which there must be a minimum time delay equal to the time of light travel." For a detailed critique, see Martin (2002, p. S227).

My approach here speaks to a third category of concerns, that the gauge argument is awkwardly placed as an argument for a quantum theory of electromagnetism. Here too I agree with Wallace:

> In fact, it seems to me that the standard argument feels convincing only because, when using it, we forget what the wavefunction really is [i.e. a wavefunction on configuration space]. It is not a complex classical field on spacetime, yet the standard argument, in effect, assumes that it is. This in turn suggests that the true home of the gauge argument is not non-relativistic quantum mechanics, but classical field theory. (Wallace, 2009, p. 211)

In Section 2.2, we will switch perspectives from the *verdammten Quanten-springerei* to the context of classical Lagrangian field theory, and propose a framework that substantially clarifies the roles of global gauge symmetries, of local gauge symmetries, and of their relationship, which I will call the "Noether gauge argument."

2.2 A Noether Reason for Gauge

In Section 2.2.1 I will set out the pre-requisite assumptions necessary for my argument based on Noether's theorems. Then, in Section 2.2.2 I will set up the mathematical background and equations that will be analyzed in a case-by-case basis in the subsections of Section 2.2.3.

2.2.1 Overview

For a more general view of how gauge symmetries constrain the dynamics of a physical theory, I will now, as announced in Section 2.1.2, make a two-step use of the theorems of Emmy Noether (1918): the first, and then the second. I will refer to this as the *Noether gauge argument*. Agreed: this is by no means a new observation, since practicing physicists use this property of gauge frequently![7] But I believe it is worth highlighting and clarifying exactly the kind of information that can be extracted in various cases, as part of my advocacy that philosophical discussions of gauge should better recognize gauge's significance for theory construction.

To recall the sketch of the argument: the Noether gauge argument proceeds in two steps. First, we choose a rigid gauge symmetry associated with an arbitrary global gauge group, and propose that its action produces a variational symmetry: by Noether's first theorem, this guarantees the presence of a collection of conserved quantities. But matter fields do not exist in isolation: they couple to

---

[7] A succinct example in a recent discussion of Noether's second theorem (Avery & Schwab, 2016), writes, "Noether's second theorem, which constrains the general structure of theories with local symmetry".

other "force" fields. Thus, in the second step, we introduce such a field and apply Noether's second theorem, "loosening" the rigid global symmetries to local, malleable ones.

About the generality and applicability of Noether's theorems, there are several issues that I will not address, but which should bridle undue enthusiasm (cf. Brown (2022)). First, Noether's theorems apply only to those theories that admit a Lagrangian (variational) formulation. But there are mathematical models that are useful and which do not admit such a formulation: Fourier's heat equation and Navier-Stokes equations are well-known examples. Second, if one takes the equations of motion and not the Lagrangian as fundamental, there are many Lagrangians that give the same equations of motion, and there is, in general no unique symmetry associated with a given conservation law, or vice versa; (though most of these ambiguities can be accounted for by different boundary terms or boundary conditions, which don't affect the fundamental meaning of the conservation law). Third, the meaning of the conserved quantity obtained from a given symmetry could be theory dependent. For instance, one can obtain a conserved quantity associated with time translation symmetry for a damped oscillator, but this is not energy as usually construed (for nondamped systems). There is also the matter of explanatory priority between conservation laws and symmetries, which I will not address here.

Thus, I will not only assume the minimum conditions under which the theorems apply, but in the interest of clarity and pedagogy, I will make several simplifying assumptions, both about the Lagrangian density and about the action of the gauge group, some of which are not strictly speaking necessary but which simplify my argument. So there are mathematically more general and more abstract ways to formulate this argument (see e.g. Gomes (2022)), but for our analysis, it is worthwhile to be specific about the field content of the theory, and show how local, or malleable symmetries provide three concrete constraints on the dynamics (namely, the vanishing of the three lines in Equation (2.2.8)). The interpretation of these constraints can be seen on a case-by-case, or sector-by-sector, basis: we will consider their implications for global versus local symmetries, as well as for theories that contain a force field that transforms under the transformation versus those that contain no such force field. Thus in the following sections we will spell out the consequences of the three constraints for four different sectors of the theory.[8]

Throughout this discussion, I will follow standard practice and distinguish two equivalence relations for classical fields on a manifold. First, I will write

---

[8] The formalism equally applies to spin-2, or gravitational, fields; but, apart from some cursory remarks, we will not discuss these.

"=" to denote ordinary equality between fields, irrespective of the satisfaction of the equations of motion, and refer to this as *strong* or *off-shell* equality. Second, given a fixed Lagrangian, I will write "≈" to denote equality between fields that holds if the Euler-Lagrange equations are satisfied for that Lagrangian, and refer to this as *weak* or *on-shell* equality.[9]

2.2.2 Mathematical Setup*

Now I will introduce, without much explanation, some of the mathematical objects that will be the focus of Section 3. Here, the reader should just take the definitions at face value: they will be explained and motivated in that section.

We start by assuming that φ is some field on spacetime, whose dynamically possible models are determined by a Lagrangian scalar function $L(\varphi) \in C^{\infty}(M)$, as those that extremize the integral of this function over M (called the *action functional*), a condition which we write as:[10]

$$\delta \int_M L(\varphi) = 0. \tag{2.2.1}$$

Using Leibniz-linearity of δ, Equivalently, after successive integration by parts, we isolate $\delta\varphi$ and write the conditions (2.2.1) as yielding equations of motion, up to boundary terms:

$$\delta L = \mathsf{EL} \cdot \delta\varphi + d\theta(\delta\varphi), \tag{2.2.2}$$

where EL is the Euler-Lagrange functional (the left-hand part of the Euler-Lagrange equations) which has one component for each direction of $\delta\varphi$, and θ is a linear operator on variations of the fields, but it is a differential form of codimension one on spacetime (i.e. it is a boundary term).[11]

Suppose that, for any value of φ, there is a family of transformations $\delta_\xi\varphi$, whose parameters ξ form an algebra, which is such that $\delta_\xi\delta_{\xi'}\varphi - \delta_{\xi'}\delta_\xi\varphi =$

---

[9]   This common terminology is due to Dirac (cf. Henneaux & Teitelboim, 1992).

[10] The most geometric way to understand this equation is to think of L as a scalar function on the space of models, and find the models where the gradient of this function vanishes.

[11] There are a couple of comments regarding the uniqueness of the several terms involved in (2.2.2) that we should address. First, for a fixed Lagrangian, the boundary term θ has an ambiguity: $\theta \to \theta + d\kappa$, where κ is an arbitrary form of codimension two on spacetime. Second, there may be more than one Lagrangian that yields the same Euler-Lagrange part of the equations; the most common examples involve addition of terms to L that don't depend on the fields (so that their variation vanishes), and additions that amount to a general shift of the boundary term $\theta \to \theta'$, which are hard to quantify. Here I will assume the Lagrangian is fixed up to boundary terms by further requirements that are left implicit (such as locality and, in the few cases in which that is not enough to eliminate unwanted alternatives, the vaguer "simplicity" constraint).

$\delta_{[\xi,\xi']}\varphi,$[12] and so that $\delta_\xi L = 0$. So from (2.2.2):

$$\delta_\xi L = \mathrm{EL} \cdot \delta_\xi \varphi + \mathrm{d}\theta_\xi = 0, \tag{2.2.3}$$

and so, for dynamically possible models, for which $\mathrm{EL} = 0$, we get

$$\mathrm{d}\theta_\xi \approx 0, \tag{2.2.4}$$

where θ_ξ is the *Noether charge* associated to the symmetry ξ, and where $\theta_\xi :=$ $\theta(\delta_\xi\varphi)$. The Noether charge inherits the ambiguity $\theta \rightarrow \theta + \mathrm{d}\kappa$ in the boundary term, but the ambiguity does not matter for conserved quantities, since $\mathrm{d}\circ\mathrm{d} = 0$ (or, equivalently, the boundary of a boundary is empty: $\partial\partial B = \emptyset$).

Noether's second theorem also follows from (2.2.3). Assume that the symmetries are malleable, or local, so that we can restrict to those ξ such that $\xi_{|B} = 0$. Now, there are inner products $\langle\bullet,\bullet\rangle$ and $\langle\langle\bullet,\bullet\rangle\rangle$, on the appropriate function spaces of φ and ξ, respectively, so that

$$\delta_\xi \int L(\varphi) = \int \mathrm{EL} \cdot \delta_\xi\varphi = \int \langle\mathrm{EL}, \delta_\xi\varphi\rangle = \int \langle\langle\Delta^\dagger\mathrm{EL}, \xi\rangle\rangle = 0 \tag{2.2.5}$$

where $\Delta^\dagger$ is the formal adjoint of $\delta_\xi\varphi$, seen as a linear operator on ξ (see Fischer & Marsden (1979) for a thorough, geometric formulation of such inner products and adjoints in the space of fields of gauge theory and general relativity). Since (2.2.3) must vanish for all such ξ, it implies a local equation that the Euler-Lagrange equations must satisfy everywhere, and which is valid off-shell:

$$\Delta^\dagger\mathrm{EL} = 0. \tag{2.2.6}$$

Because these constraints are valid off-shell, they reflect a kinematic property of the variables of the theory. For instance, the Bianchi identities for the curvature tensors (which applies both to (semi-)Riemannian geometry and principal fiber bundles; cf. Proposition 4 in "The Curvature" section) is a purely geometric property that will give rise to such constraints. These are geometrical identities, that tell us that not all components of the curvature tensors are independent: they satisfy differential and algebraic constraints. In all theories under consideration here, local, covariant tensors that involve derivatives of the fundamental variables – either the gauge potential or the metric – must be written in terms of curvature (cf. e.g. Lovelock (1972)), and so obey such geometric constraints. Thus, the equations of motion obtained from Lagrangians that involve

---

[12] This condition is important in order to ensure that the symmetry-related values of the fields form an "orbit," or an integral submanifold in the space of models of the theory. The condition assumes that ξ does not depend on φ: for the full explication of these equations in terms of the geometry of the space of models, and a generalization to the case where ξ is model-dependent, see Gomes et al. (2019); Gomes & Riello (2021).

derivatives of the fundamental variables, will in some way or another inherit these constraints and so cannot all be independent. In other words, there are more independent variables than there are equations of motion. For this reason such equations of motion cannot be used to *uniquely* determine the evolution of all the fundamental variables: they do so only for a constrained subset. I will get back to this topic in Section 5.3.1, when we discuss non-locality.

Now let us be more specific. Let us start with the material charges, which I will represent as fields with no spacetime index, but, assuming the value space is a vector space V, with indices a; so that $\psi^a(x) \in V$ for $x \in M$, where M is spacetime and V is a vector space. In relativity, M is a smooth Lorentzian manifold, that is, equipped with a nondegenerate symmetric bilinear product that is not positive definite, having a signature of $(3, 1)$. To simplify the notation, when discussing gauge theory, I'll consider the case of a Minkowski metric, whose Levi-Civita covariant derivative I'll denote as ∂ (the generalization to another metric would amount to a minimal replacement $\partial \rightarrow \nabla$). From the pragmatic, nongeometric standpoint of this section, assume that the symmetries associated to the conservation of charges arise from the action of a Lie group, G on V (cf. footnote 5). We define this action pointwise as $g \cdot \psi(x) = g(x) \cdot \psi(x) \in V$. Let t_I^{ij} be the n-dimensional Hermitean matrix representation on V of $\mathfrak{g}$, that is, $t : \mathfrak{g} \rightarrow GL(V)$, where the I are indices of the Lie algebra space, in the domain of the map, and i,j denote the matrix indices in the image of the map, acting linearly on V.[13]

I will also assume that the forces that are sourced by ψ have direction in space – as forces are prone to have – and take value again in some internal vector space. For reasons to be clarified in Section 3, at this point I will take these value spaces as being linearly isomorphic to the Lie algebra: so the force fields are labeled A_μ^I, they take vectors of M to $\mathfrak{g}$, with μ representing the spacetime components of the vector.[14] These fields are associated with a dynamics by postulating a real-valued action functional $S(\psi_i, A_\mu^I)$, whose extremal values provide the equations of motion.

We take the (malleable, or local) gauge transformations, infinitesimally parametrized by $\xi \in \mathfrak{g}$, to act on our fundamental variables as:

---

[13] These assumptions will only be justified in Sections 3 and 4.

[14] In brief: there must be a faithful, irreducible action of the Lie group on the force fields; this means that the operative part of the force field will be isomorphic to the Lie algebra. What is a "force" and what is "matter" are distinguished by their transformation properties under a gauge transformation. Matter transforms linearly, whereas forces acquire derivatives of the generator as inhomogeneous terms. The simplest explanation for this is that the force fields encode the interior geometry of a more structured space, as we will see in Section 3.

$$\begin{cases} \delta_\xi \psi_i = \xi^I t_I^{ij} \psi_j = (\xi t \psi)_i \\ \delta_\xi A_\mu^I = D_\mu \xi^I = \partial_\mu \xi^I + [\xi, A_\mu]^I \end{cases} \qquad (2.2.7)$$

where the square brackets are the Lie algebra commutators (again, we will justify these transformations in Section 3). These transformation rules are not as general as they could be, but neither are they arbitrary: they are highly constrained by the theory of representations of Lie groups on vector spaces! But even without going into representation theory, the reader can recognize that these are the first-order terms of the Lie algebra action on the respective vector spaces – in particular, "first-order" in the derivatives of ξ and in powers of A and ψ – and in this sense provide an appropriate approximation of any malleable gauge transformation.

Our aim now is to constrain how the matter fields ψ couple to force fields. Let $\mathcal{L}(\psi, \partial\psi, A, \partial A)$ be the Lagrangian defining our action $S(\psi, A)$, which we assume for simplicity does not depend on derivatives of higher order than two.[15] Variation along the directions of the gauge transformations previously yields (with summation convention on all indices):

$$\left(\frac{\delta\mathcal{L}}{\delta\psi_i}(t^I \psi)_i + \frac{\delta\mathcal{L}}{\delta\partial_\mu\psi_i}(t^I \partial_\mu\psi)_i + \left[\frac{\delta\mathcal{L}}{\delta A_\nu}, A_\nu \right]^I + \left[\frac{\delta\mathcal{L}}{\delta\partial_\nu A_\mu}, \partial_\mu A_\nu \right]^I \right) \xi_I +$$

$$\left(\frac{\delta\mathcal{L}}{\delta\partial_\mu\psi_i}(t^I \psi)_i + \frac{\delta\mathcal{L}}{\delta A_\mu^I} + \left[\frac{\delta\mathcal{L}}{\delta\partial_\nu A_\mu}, A_\nu \right]^I \right) \partial_\mu\xi_I + \qquad (2.2.8)$$

$$\frac{\delta\mathcal{L}}{\delta\partial_\nu A_\mu^I} \partial_\mu\partial_\nu\xi^I = 0$$

Since the derivatives of ξ are functionally independent, this equation implies that *each line must vanish separately*: the first line is a consequence of global symmetries – the equation would have to be satisfied even if the symmetry was independent of the spacetime point – and the remaining two are consequences of local symmetries. These are the fundamental constraints on the dynamics that we propose to analyze, and the task of the remainder of this section will be to unpack them.

The requirement that each of these lines vanishes provides a strong constraint on the form of the Lagrangian, and hence on the dynamics. This, I claim, provides the core of the Noether gauge argument.

---

[15] This can be justified by appeal to Ostrogradsky's theorem; see Swanson (2019) for a philosophical discussion.

2.2.3 The Four Different Cases

To extract interesting physical information from the constraint given by (2.2.8), there are four sectors to compare, arising from the use of either global or local symmetries, and either A-independent or A-dependent Lagrangians. We treat each sector in turn.

The results will be: when A does not figure in the Lagrangian, a theory with global symmetries can be dynamically nontrivial and complete. In such a theory the charges don't couple to forces, so it will not require further constraints for consistency. With local symmetries and no A-dependence, the constraints demand that the dynamics be trivial, that is, no kinetic term for the matter field can appear in the Lagrangian. When forces have their own dynamics, that is, when the Lagrangian is A-dependent, a theory with global symmetries may be incomplete, and require further constraints to render the dynamics of A compatible with charge conservation; an example will be given. It is only in the last case, where we have local symmetries and A-dependence, that the equations of motion coupling forces to charges is automatically consistent with the conservation of charges (and so no further constraints are required). Thus, we will see the power of malleable symmetries and A-dependence together to secure an interacting dynamics that conserves charge. And this will be our Noether gauge argument.

Force-Independent Lagrangian, with Global Symmetries

First, suppose we are as in the first step of the textbook gauge argument: there is no A in sight, and the symmetry is global, so that $\partial_\mu \xi^I = 0 = \partial_\mu \partial_\nu \xi^I$. Then the vanishing of the first line of Equation (2.2.8) reduces to

$$\frac{\delta \mathcal{L}}{\delta \psi_i}(t^I \psi)_i + \frac{\delta \mathcal{L}}{\delta \partial_\mu \psi_i}(t^I \partial_\mu \psi)_i = 0. \tag{2.2.9}$$

But by the Euler-Lagrange equations $\mathsf{EL}(\psi)_i \approx 0$, where $\mathsf{EL}(\psi)_i = \frac{\delta \mathcal{L}}{\delta \psi_i} - \partial_\mu \frac{\delta \mathcal{L}}{\delta \partial_\mu \psi_i}$, we have

$$\frac{\delta \mathcal{L}}{\delta \psi_i} \approx \partial_\mu \frac{\delta \mathcal{L}}{\delta \partial_\mu \psi_i}, \tag{2.2.10}$$

where we again are using "$\approx$" to denote "on-shell" equality. Applying this to Equation (2.2.9) we find that

$$\partial_\mu \left(\frac{\delta \mathcal{L}}{\delta \partial_\mu \psi_i}(t^I \psi)_i \right) = \partial^\mu J_\mu^I(\psi) \approx 0 \tag{2.2.11}$$

where we have defined the part that is conserved as the matter current:

$$J^j_\mu(\psi) := \frac{\delta \mathcal{L}}{\delta \partial_\mu \psi_i}(t^j \psi)_i, \tag{2.2.12}$$

as is customary.

In summary, we have derived what is guaranteed by Noether's first theorem, that the current $J^j_\mu(\psi)$ is conserved on-shell. Or, turning this around: symmetry requires the Lagrangian to be restricted so that $J^j_\mu(\psi)$ defined in Equation (2.2.12) is divergenceless. Having constrained the space of theories in this manner, there are no more equations to satisfy: conservation of charge is consistent with the dynamics and no further constraints need to be imposed.

Force-Independent Lagrangian, with Local Symmetries

In the next case, suppose that we allow – in addition to "Force-independent Lagrangian, with global symmetries" section's equations – the ones arising from a $\partial \xi \neq 0$, while still not allowing for an A in the theory. We get, in addition to equations (2.2.12) and (2.2.11), from the vanishing of the second line of Equation (2.2.8):

$$\frac{\delta \mathcal{L}}{\delta \partial_\mu \psi_i}(t^j \psi)_i = J^j_\mu(\psi) = 0. \tag{2.2.13}$$

So here the conserved currents are forced to vanish. Clearly this condition is guaranteed for all field values if $\frac{\delta \mathcal{L}}{\delta \partial_\mu \psi_i} = 0$, which requires a vanishing kinetic term. A careful analysis of more general cases reveals this is the only generic solution.[16]

This analysis pinpoints the obstacle appearing in the textbook gauge argument that we rehearsed in Section 2.1.1. When the matter field Lagrangian has a nontrivial kinetic term, local transformations cannot be variational symmetries. That is: if we impose local symmetries without introducing a gauge potential, we cannot consistently also allow a term in the Lagrangian including $\partial_\mu \psi_i$. It is to allow such terms and still retain the local symmetries that the next two sections will introduce the gauge potential.

---

[16] For instance, assume $\frac{\delta \mathcal{L}}{\delta \partial_\mu \psi_i}$ depends only on $\partial_\mu \psi_i$, then since $t^j_{ij} \psi^i$ can take any value, we must have $\frac{\delta \mathcal{L}}{\delta \partial_\mu \psi_i} = 0$. Now, suppose $\frac{\delta \mathcal{L}}{\delta \partial_\mu \psi_i}$ depends on ψ_i as well. Since ψ_i has no spacetime indices to match the μ of the gradient $\partial_\mu \psi_i$, to make a Lagrangian scalar, we would need the ψ_i contribution to this term to itself be a scalar, call it $\mathcal{F}(\psi)$. So for example: $\frac{\delta \mathcal{L}}{\delta \partial_\mu \psi_i} = \partial_\mu \psi_i(\psi_j \psi^j)$, or more generally $\frac{\delta \mathcal{L}}{\delta \partial_\mu \psi_i} = \mathcal{F}'(\partial \psi)_{i\mu} F(\psi)$ (where we raise indices with an inner product of $\mathcal{F}$); and as in the example $\mathcal{F}(\psi) = \psi_j \psi^j = 0$ iff $\psi = 0$. But then the same argument as before suffices, since we can still allow $t^j_{ij} \psi^i$ to take any value in $\mathcal{F}$ (for an appropriate, nonzero value of the scalar formed just from ψ, e.g. the contraction $\psi_j \psi^j$). Or, in other words, for $\psi \neq 0$, $\frac{\delta \mathcal{L}}{\delta \partial_\mu \psi_i}(t^j \psi)_i = 0$ iff $\mathcal{F}^{-1}(\psi) \frac{\delta \mathcal{L}}{\delta \partial_\mu \psi_i}(t^j \psi)_i = 0$ where $\mathcal{F}^{-1}(\psi) \frac{\delta \mathcal{L}}{\delta \partial_\mu \psi_i}$ depends only on $\partial_\mu \psi$; and thus we are back to the first, simple case.

Force-Dependent Lagrangian, with Global Symmetries

We first proceed precisely as in the first case, introducing the A field, but still *keeping the symmetries global*. Using the equations of motion for A as well as those of ψ, that is, EL[A] = 0 as well as EL[ψ] = 0, we get, in direct analogy to (2.2.11), a conserved current that is a sum of two currents:[17]

$$\partial_\mu \left(\frac{\delta \mathcal{L}}{\delta \partial_\mu \psi_i}(t^I \psi)_i + \left[\frac{\delta \mathcal{L}}{\delta \partial_\nu A_\mu}, A_\nu \right]^I \right) = \partial^\mu (J_\mu^I(\psi) + \tilde{J}_\mu^I(A)) \approx 0 \qquad (2.2.14)$$

and nothing more; there are no further conditions that the terms of the Lagrangian need to obey. (Here, the definition of $\tilde{J}_\mu^I(A))$ is given implicitly by (2.2.14).)

So, unlike the previous case, which admitted only a trivial kinetic term for the matter field ψ, this sector will admit many possible dynamics. The problem here is of a different nature: the theories are not sufficiently constrained; the equations of motion do not automatically guarantee conservation of charges.

Let us look at an example of how things can go wrong in this intermediate sector containing forces but only global symmetries, for the simple, Abelian theory. In the Abelian theory, $\tilde{J}(A) \equiv 0$, since quantities trivially commute. Thus, Equation (2.2.14) only contains the standard conservation of the matter charges and the symmetries are silent about the relationship between this charge and the dynamics of the forces.

Consider a kinetic term of the form $\partial_{(\mu} A_{\nu)} \partial^{(\mu} A^{\nu)}$ where round brackets denote symmetrization. So this differs from the standard Maxwell theory kinetic term for the gauge potential: namely, $V_{\mu\nu} F^{\mu\nu} := \partial_{[\mu} A_{\nu]} \partial^{[\mu} A^{\nu]}$ where square brackets denote *anti*-symmetrization. But the symmetrized version is nonetheless gauge-invariant (under *global* transformations). Now, the Euler-Lagrange equations for this theory differ only very slightly from the Maxwell-Klein-Gordon equations. The equations of motion for A yield:

$$\partial^\mu (\partial_{(\mu} A_{\nu)}) = J_\nu \qquad (2.2.15)$$

in contrast with the usual $\partial^\mu (\partial_{[\mu} A_{\nu]}) = J_\nu$. But while the divergence of the right-hand side automatically vanishes, unlike the usual case the divergence of the left-hand side does not:

$$\partial^\nu \partial^\mu (\partial_{(\mu} A_{\nu)}) = \partial^\mu \partial_\mu \partial^\nu A_\nu = \Box \partial^\nu A_\nu \neq 0. \qquad (2.2.16)$$

---

[17] To be explicit, the A-dependent terms that appear in the first line of (2.2.8) are $\left[\frac{\delta \mathcal{L}}{\delta A_\nu}, A_\nu \right]^I +$ $\left[\frac{\delta \mathcal{L}}{\delta \partial_\nu A_\mu}, \partial_\mu A_\nu \right]^I \approx \left[\partial_\mu \frac{\delta \mathcal{L}}{\delta \partial_\nu A_\mu}, A_\nu \right]^I + \left[\frac{\delta \mathcal{L}}{\delta \partial_\nu A_\mu}, \partial_\mu A_\nu \right]^I = \partial_\mu \left[\frac{\delta \mathcal{L}}{\delta \partial_\nu A_\mu}, A_\nu \right]^I.$

At this point, we would have to go back to the drawing board and introduce more constraints on the theory: this theory does not couple forces to charges in a manner that guarantees charge conservation.

Thus we glimpse my overall thesis: only by introducing local gauge symmetries do we restrict interactions between forces and their sources so that they are consistent with the conservation of the matter current.

Of course, in this example the culprit is easily found: the kinetic term $\partial_{(\mu}A_{\nu)}\partial^{(\mu}A^{\nu)}$ is *not* invariant under local transformations. According to the next section – our fourth sector – requiring this stronger form of invariance will restrict us to the space of consistent interactions. No tweaking required.

Force-Dependent Lagrangian, with Local Symmetries

In this fourth sector, we again obtain (2.2.14), from the vanishing of the first line of (2.2.8) – the constraint for the global symmetry – since nothing changes at that level. But, from the vanishing of the second line in Equation (2.2.8), we have:

$$-\frac{\delta\mathcal{L}}{\delta A_\mu^I} = \frac{\delta\mathcal{L}}{\delta\partial_\mu\psi_i}(t^I\psi)_i + \left[\frac{\delta\mathcal{L}}{\delta\partial_\nu A_\mu}, A_\nu\right]^I = J_\mu^I(\psi) + \tilde{J}_\mu^I(A). \qquad (2.2.17)$$

Once again using the Euler-Lagrange equations for A to substitute the left-hand side, we find that

$$\text{EL}(A)_\mu^I = \frac{\delta\mathcal{L}}{\delta A_\mu^I} - \partial_\nu\frac{\delta\mathcal{L}}{\delta\partial_\nu A_\mu^I} \approx 0. \qquad (2.2.18)$$

Defining $\frac{\delta\mathcal{L}}{\delta\partial_\nu A_\mu^I} =: k_{\mu\nu}^I$, we now obtain:

$$J_\mu^I(\psi) + \tilde{J}_\mu^I(A) = -\partial^\mu k_{\mu\nu}^I + \text{EL}(A)_\mu^I \approx -\partial^\mu k_{\mu\nu}^I \qquad (2.2.19)$$

This equation links both the matter and force currents to the dynamics of the force field, given in $\text{EL}(A)_\mu^I$.

We already know from the constraint for the global symmetry, Equation (2.2.8), that the sum of the currents is divergence-free on shell (cf. Equation 2.2.14). Thus, taking the divergence of (2.2.19), the left side vanishes, thus consistency between charge conservation and the dynamics of the force fields demand that the right-hand side must also vanish, implying that $\partial^\nu\partial^\mu k_{\mu\nu}^I = 0$. Since partial derivatives are necessarily symmetric, all we need in order to satisfy conservation is that:

$$k_{\mu\nu}^I = -k_{\nu\mu}^I \quad \text{or} \quad k_{\mu\nu}^I = k_{[\nu\mu]}^I, \qquad (2.2.20)$$

which is just what we have from the vanishing of the *third* line of Equation (2.2.8). So the condition was automatically satisfied. The result of including local symmetries, in this simple case, restricts us to consider Lagrangians in which the derivatives of A_μ^I only enter in anti-symmetrized form: $\partial_{[\mu} A_{\nu]}^I$. This restriction excludes the previous example of Equation (2.2.15).

More generally, if we try to find a Lagrangian that includes force fields without obeying the relations obtained from the local symmetries, the equations of motion of the force fields and those relating force fields and matter may require further constraints to be compatible with charge conservation, as we saw in the counter-example in the previous section. This is one superpower of local gauge symmetries: they link charge conservation – taken as empirical fact or on a priori grounds – with the form of the Lagrangian for the force fields.

3 Gauge Theory and the Geometry of Fiber Bundles

This is the section in which I introduce the standard geometric approach to gauge theory. (In Section 4, I will introduce a less standard geometric approach.)

In Section 3.1 I will motivate the use of fiber bundles without appealing to any complicated mathematics. This section will introduce the main ideas to be developed in the rest of the section in a pedagogic fashion. Section 3.2 is more mathematically advanced and gets an asterisk (*). Indeed, it is the most mathematically involved in this Element, and so it merits a further preamble. The modern mathematical formalism of gauge theories relies on the theory of principal and associated fiber bundles. I will not give a comprehensive account here (cf. e.g. Kobayashi & Nomizu (1963); Michor (2008) for rigorous mathematical treatments, Nakahara (2003) for a physics-based approach, or Baez & Munian (1994) for a more pedagogic conceptual introduction). There are also more (many more!) mathematically comprehensive sources on this topic in the literature, but I will focus only on the parts that are important for the geometric picture of gauge theory, and not get bogged down on existence proofs, and so on. For the demonstrations that are included, I will try to use more modern, shorter proofs, that as far as I know are only scattered throughout the literature. In Section 3.3 I will summarize the main ingredients that go into building a gauge theory of particles using the mathematics developed in the previous sections.

3.1 A Brief Introduction to Fiber Bundles

Our intuitive picture of a field over space or spacetime is something like temperature. A temperature field can be written as a map from space or spacetime M to the real numbers, $T : M \to \mathbb{R}$; each point in M is assigned a temperature. We want to consider fields that have a more complicated "internal structure," or "charge structure," than temperature, so we can generalize from real numbers to vectors, in which case instead of T we have $\psi : M \rightarrow V$, a map from spacetime to some vector space V.

Such a map gives us a definite identity relation for the value of the field at two different points of M. Namely, two points x, y can have the same value of temperature, or be mapped to the same element of V. We could have a less rigid structure, where, each $x \in M$ gets its own "copy" of V, with all such copies being linearly isomorphic to V, but where we leave the isomorphism unspecified.[18] This is how we implement the idea that there is no absolute comparison of elements of V belonging to different points of M. Now, an isomorphism from the copy of V over x to one over y will be given by *a parallel transport* between these two spaces, which requires further structure to be defined. In general this isomorphism may depend on the path taken from x to y. Fields then correspond to a particular assignment of one value $v_x \in V$ per point $x \in M$: these are called *sections* of the vector bundle over M with typical fiber V.

One example of such vector spaces V is familiar from differential geometry: namely, from the tangent bundle TM, whose elements are, at each point, tangent to curves that pass through that point and are such that $T_x M \simeq \mathbb{R}^4 = V$, for a four-dimensional spacetime, where here $\simeq$ represents a linear isomorphism that is not canonically specified.[19] Indeed, even if TM were globally trivializable, so that a product structure could be found for its totality: $TM \simeq M \times \mathbb{R}^4$, this would not mean we could identify an element $v \in \mathbb{R}^4$ at different points of M, because such an identification would depend on the choice of isomorphism between $T_x M \simeq \mathbb{R}^4$.

Because the elements of $T_x M$ correspond to tangent of curves passing through x, we say the tangent bundle is a vector bundle that is "soldered" onto spacetime. But the fields employed in modern theoretical physics – representing different properties of matter – live in more general vector bundles than TM, and are not soldered to spacetime.

These "charged fields" have components at each spacetime point that are not associated to spacetime directions; they represent degrees of freedom that are "internal": think of it as a "color" or as a kind of charge. Such charged matter

---

[18] There are many reasons for this extension; here are two. First, we can think of mathematical objects which associate a linear vector space to each point but that, even topologically, don't admit a description as a product space, $M \times V$. For instance, inspired by the Möbius strip, we can construct a line bundle which associates a real line to each point of S^1, but which "flips" the line when the circle closes. Second, once we start thinking operationally of "dragging" an element of V over x along a curve, it is natural to let this dragging depend on the curve, and not just on the final points.

[19] There are other ways of thinking of tangent vectors, for example, as derivative operators; cf Boothby (2010).

fields interact through fundamental forces other than the gravitational force, and each of these forces is related to a given symmetry group. The forces tell us how the charge value at one spacetime point gets dragged along a spacetime curve to another charge value at another spacetime point.

The main idea underlying the physical significance of the parallel transport of internal quantities was already well stated in the paper that introduced this mathematical machinery into physics, Yang and Mills (1954):

> The conservation of isotopic spin is identical with the requirement of invariance of all interactions under isotopic spin rotation. This means that when electromagnetic interactions can be neglected, as we shall hereafter assume to be the case, the orientation of the isotopic spin is of no physical significance. The differentiation between a neutron and a proton is then a purely arbitrary process. As usually conceived, however, this arbitrariness is subject to the following limitation: once one chooses what to call a proton, what a neutron, at one space-time point, one is then not free to make any choices at other space-time points.

The idea here is that calling a particle a proton or a neutron at a given point is meaningless; only *relational* or, more broadly, *structural* properties of the theory can have physical significance, for instance, whether your original "proton" became a "neutron" upon going around a loop.[20] The only physically relevant information is a notion of sameness across different points of spacetime: thus, once we label a given particle as, for example, a proton at one point of spacetime, the structure of the bundle specifies what would also count as a proton at another spacetime point, infinitesimally nearby. In Section 3.2, we give the technical conditions that make precise this idea.

3.2 Fiber Bundles in Gauge Theory

This is a rather long section, and more mathematically involved than the others. But I will start slow, in Section 3.2.1, providing more motivation for using fiber bundles in general, and then principal fiber bundles and their associated vector bundles. As I mentioned previously, the basic idea of a bundle is that it has internal spaces associates with each spacetime point – called fibers – and there is no canonical way to identify points in different fibers. I will introduce fibers that are vector spaces, and then will try to give some intuition for principal fiber bundles as bundles of linear frames for these vector spaces. In Section 3.2.2 I will develop the promised mathematical machinery, with particular attention to conceptual elements.

---

[20] Of course, this example, which originally motivated Yang and Mills, applies only in the context of isospin symmetry – which is approximate. For the electric charge tells protons and neutron apart in an intrinsic manner.

3.2.1 The Intuition Behind Fiber Bundles

To gather intuition about principal fiber bundles (PFBs) as the "organizers" of symmetry principles, as described in Section 3.1, it is worthwhile to introduce them in the context of the familiar tangent vector fields on M.

Fiber bundles are spaces that locally look like a product; that is, they form a 'bundle' of fibers over a base manifold (usually spacetime). Let us denote fiber bundles by E; they are smooth manifolds that admit the action of a surjective projection $\pi_E : E \to M$ so that any point of M has a neighborhood, $U \subset M$, such that E is locally of the form $\pi_E^{-1}(U) \simeq U \times V$, where V, as previously, is isomorphic to some "fiber": a space over each point of M and in which the fields take their values, and similarly for all subsets of U, which ensures that $\pi_E^{-1}(x) \simeq V$. But the isomorphism between $\pi_E^{-1}(U)$ and $U \times V$ is not unique, which is why there is no canonical identification of elements of fibers over different points of spacetime. Each choice of isomorphism is called "a trivialization" of the bundle: it is basically a coordinate system that makes the local product structure explicit. It is standard to denote a fiber bundle E over M, with typical fiber V, with the triple (E, M, V).

Definition 1 (A section of a bundle) *A field-configuration for E is called a section, and it is a map $\kappa : U \to E$ such that $\pi_E \circ \kappa = \mathrm{Id}_U$. We denote smooth sections like this by $\kappa \in \Gamma(E)$.*[21]

Sections replace the functions $\tilde{\kappa} : M \to V$, that we would employ if the fields had a fixed, or "absolute" – that is, spacetime independent – space of values.

There are essentially two kinds of bundles that we will encounter here: a vector bundle and a principal fiber bundle; a third type, *an associated vector bundle*, is a vector bundle that is associated to a principal bundle.

Each matter field in a gauge theory is described by a section on a vector bundle, corresponding to that field. Indeed, given a vector bundle E over M (which we will describe next in more depth), we can directly define an affine connection D as:

$$D : \Gamma(E) \to \Gamma(T^*M \otimes E) \tag{3.2.1}$$

such that the product rule

$$D(fs) = df \otimes s + f Ds \tag{3.2.2}$$

---

[21] It is somewhat confusing that a *section of a vector bundle* is different from the section of a principal bundle, which we will discuss next. So, for instance two different configurations of the electron field are two different sections of its vector bundle, and thus are not counted as "equivalent" in the way that two sections of a principal bundle are. And while a global section of P exists iff the bundle is trivial, we can always find a global section of an associated bundle (cf. Kobayashi & Nomizu (1963, Theo. 5.7)).

is satisfied for all smooth, real (or complex)-valued functions f. But then the reader should ask: aren't we essentially done? If we can define a covariant derivative for different matter fields directly, why introduce any other kind of bundle, what further structure do we need, for example, in order to write down a Lagrangian?

The problem, as it stands, is that each vector bundle has its own covariant derivative, and so the covariant derivatives of different matter fields are "unco-ordinated." Without such a coordination, covariant derivatives of different, but interacting fields would not "march-in-step." This would imply that the notion of relative "charge," for example, of electric charge of different matter fields, would be extremely history dependent, and unhelpful. The role of principal and associated bundle is to provide a mechanism for the coordination of covariant derivative among fields that have charges of the same type. In other words, associated vector bundles inherit their covariant derivatives from a single prin-cipal bundle, and so, if we tie each force to a principal bundle, we solve this coordination problem. I will discuss this further in Section 4.

Two Examples of Bundles

Example of a vector bundle: the tangent bundle. The tangent bundle, TM serves again to illustrate these constructions. A smooth tangent vector field is a smooth assignment of elements of TM over M, in this case it is usual to, instead of κ, use the notation $X \in \Gamma(TM)$, with $\pi_{TM} : TM \to M$, mapping $X_x \in T_xM \to x \in M$. The tangent bundle TM *locally* has the form of a product space, $U \times V$, with $V \simeq \mathbb{R}^4$.

Example of a principal bundle: the bundle of frames of the tangent bundle. We can build a principal bundle as the set of all linear frames of TM, called "the frame bundle" (where "frame" means "basis of the tangent space T_xM"), written $L(TM)$. The fiber over each point of the base space M consists of all choices $\{e_i(x)\}_{i=1,\cdots 4} \in L(TM)$, of sets of spanning and linearly indepen-dent vectors (here the index I enumerates the basis elements); and there is a one-to-one map between the group $GL(\mathbb{R}^4)$ and the fiber: we can use the group to go from any frame to any other (at that same point), but there is no basis that canonically corresponds to $\mathrm{Id} \in GL(\mathbb{R}^4)$. Similarly, given any vector bundle E with typical fiber V, the bundle of frames $L(E)$ forms a principal fiber bundle with $GL(V)$ as the structure group.

This example illustrates a feature of principal fiber bundles that distinguishes them from vector bundles: the fibers of a principal bundle can be mapped 1-1 not to a vector space but to a Lie group G, and since the fibers have no preferred identity element, they are isomorphic to G only as a homogeneous space.

Parallel Transport

We can now use this principal bundle to "coordinate" the parallel transport of different tensor fields.[22]

The bundle of frames is perfect for illustrating, in a familiar setting, how parallel transport is encoded by connections in principal fiber bundles. Directions transversal to the fiber will relate frames over neighboring points of M; they will tell us which basis over $x + \delta x$ corresponds to a chosen basis over $x \in M$. Imagining the manifold M to lie horizontally on the page, we think of the fibers as vertical, and, on P, we dub as *horizontal* a preferred set of directions transversal to the fibers, that we take as a preferential link between the frames on neighboring fibers. The horizontal space at a point is isomorphic to the tangent space of the base manifold under that point: $H_p \simeq T_{\pi(p)}M$ (cf. next subsection). So, the vertical spaces – the fibers – are part of the basic structure of the principal bundle, but a preferred choice of a transversal distribution – called horizontal – is not. Indeed, in physical theories, the principal bundle will be the fixed background on which the horizontal distribution is dynamical.

Thus, in the frame bundles, a horizontal direction at a point determines which frames in neighboring fibers correspond to each other, or are parallel transported. By expanding a vector field in these frames, the parallel transport of the vector fields is straightforwardly defined by constancy of the components of the vector in that parallel transported frame.

Now we will see precisely how these definitions fit together, and how we can understand entire machinery of gauge theory geometrically.

3.2.2 The Mathematics of Principal Bundles*

A principal fiber bundle is, in short, just a manifold where some group acts, and whose equivalence classes under the group action correspond 1-1 to points of spacetime. In detail:

Definition 2 (a Principal Fiber Bundle) *is a smooth manifold P that admits a smooth free action of a (path-connected, semi-simple) Lie group, G: that is, there is a map $G \times P \to P$ with $(g,p) \mapsto g \cdot p$ for some left action $\cdot$ and such that for each $p \in P$, the isotropy group is the identity (i.e. $G_p := \{g \in G \mid g \cdot p = p\} = \{e\}$).*

---

[22] But this example is deficient in one way, which we will clarify in Section 4: in order to describe the parallel transport of tensor fields we don't *need* to use the bundle of frames of TM. That is because in that case we are only looking at vector bundles of the form $E \otimes E \otimes \ldots \otimes E^* \otimes E^*$, for $E = TM$. But the formalism is flexible enough so that we can have vector bundles E and $\tilde{E}$ that are not so constructed, and yet are associated to the same principal bundle, as we will see in the next section.

Naturally, we construct a projection $\pi : P \to M$ onto equivalence classes, given by $p \sim q \Leftrightarrow p = g \cdot q$ for some $g \in G$. That is: the base space M is the orbit space of P, $M = P/G$, with the quotient topology; that is, it is characterized by an open and continuous $\pi : P \to M$.[23] By definition, G acts transitively on each fiber, that is, on each orbit of the group. Here, unlike in the general definition of a fiber bundle, we don't need to postulate the local product structure: $\pi^{-1}(U) \simeq U \times G$; it is easy to prove that this follows from Definition 2 (see the section "Local sections" for the proof).

The automorphism group of P are *fiber-preserving* diffeomorphisms, that is:

Definition 3 *Diffeomorphisms*

$$\tau : P \to P \quad \text{such that} \quad \tau(g \cdot p) = g \cdot \tau(p). \tag{3.2.3}$$

Vertical automorphisms are those fiber-preserving diffeomorphisms for which $\pi \circ \tau = \pi$; that is, they are purely "vertical" automorphisms of the bundle.

But to link fibers, we need to postulate more structure than just P: we need a connection.

The Ehresmann Connection-Form

Given an element ξ of the Lie-algebra $\mathfrak{g}$, and the action of G on P, we use the exponential to find an action of $\mathfrak{g}$ on P. This defines an embedding of the Lie algebra into the tangent space at each point, given by the *hash* operator: $\#_p : \mathfrak{g} \to T_pP$. The image of this embedding we call *the vertical space* V_p at a point $p \in P$: it is tangent to the orbits of the group, and is linearly spanned by vectors of the form

$$\text{for} \quad \xi \in \mathfrak{g}: \quad \xi^{\#}(p) := \frac{d}{dt}|_{t=0}(\exp(t\xi) \cdot p) \in V_p \subset T_pP. \tag{3.2.4}$$

Vector fields of the form $\xi^{\#}$ for $\xi \in \mathfrak{g}$ are called *fundamental vector fields*.[24]

The vertical spaces are defined canonically from the group action, as in (3.2.4). But we can define an "orthogonal" projection operator, $\widehat{V}$ such that:

$$\widehat{V}|_V = \mathsf{Id}|_V, \quad \widehat{V} \circ \widehat{V} = \widehat{V}, \tag{3.2.5}$$

and defining $H \subset TP$ as $H := \ker(\widehat{V})$. It follows that $\widehat{H} = \mathsf{Id} - \widehat{V}$ and so $\widehat{V} \circ \widehat{H} = \widehat{H} \circ \widehat{V} = 0$.[25] Moreover, since $\pi_* \circ \widehat{V} = 0$ it follows that:

---

[23] For convenience, I have dropped the subscript on the projections for principal fiber bundles.

[24] It is important to note that there are vector fields that are vertical and yet are not fundamental, since they may depend on $x \in M$ (or on the orbit).

[25] Indeed, given any vector bundle, we have a similar definition of covariant derivative that bypasses the principal bundle formalism, as in (3.2.2). In other words, following the idea that

$$\pi_* \circ \widehat{H} = \pi_*. \tag{3.2.6}$$

As I said in the previous section, the connection-form should be visualized essentially as the projection onto the vertical spaces: given some infinitesimal direction, or change of frames, the vertical projection picks out the part of that change that was due solely to a different choice of frames, and the connection-form tells us what that change of frame was. The only difference between $\widehat{V}$ and ω is that the latter is $\mathfrak{g}$-valued, Thus we get it via the isomorphism between V_p and $\mathfrak{g}$ (ω's inverse is $\# : \mathfrak{g} \mapsto V \subset TP$).

One often defines the connection directly, without appeal to vertical spaces:

Definition 4 (An Ehresmann connection-form) ω *is defined as a Lie-algebra valued one form on P, satisfying the following properties:*

$$\omega(\xi^\#) = \xi \quad\quad and \quad\quad L_g^* \omega = \mathrm{Ad}_g \omega, \tag{3.2.7}$$

where the adjoint representation of G on $\mathfrak{g}$ *is defined as* $\mathrm{Ad}_g \xi = g \xi g^{-1}$, *for* $\xi \in \mathfrak{g}$; L_g^* *is the pull-back of TP induced by the diffeomorphism* $g : P \to P$.

But it is possible to show that

Proposition 1 *A Lie-algebra-valued one form on P satisfies (3.2.7) if and only if* $\omega = \#^{-1} \circ \widehat{V}$ *(where* $\#^{-1}$ *is only defined in the restriction to the vertical subspace* $V \subset TP$*).*

The relationship between the connection, the Lie-algebra, and the vertical projection is illustrated in Figure 2.

If, on the second condition in (3.2.7), we take the infinitesimal pull-back, we get the Lie derivative along a vector $\xi^\#$ on the left-hand side, and a Lie-algebra commutator on the right-hand side, that is,

$$\mathcal{L}_{\xi^\#} \omega = [\omega, \xi]. \tag{3.2.8}$$

This equation is only valid for fundamental vector fields, $\xi^\#$. But a vertical field may be vertical without being fundamental: we could take different $\xi \in \mathfrak{g}$ at different orbits (as discussed in footnote 24), that is, $Z_p^v := (\xi(\pi(p))^\#)_p \in T_p P$, which we abbreviate to $(\xi(x)^\#)_p$. The Lie derivative in (3.2.8) is not C^∞-linear on $\xi^\#$, and so we expect some difference when we compute $\mathcal{L}_{\xi(x)^\#} \omega$. To see what that is, we first define the inner derivative (or alternating contraction

---

a connection should relate elements of neighboring fibers, we label as 'vertical' the tangent space to $\pi_E^{-1}(x)$, that is, the tangent space to E_p, seen as a subspace of TE (generated by curves in E_p), which is also canonical. So here too, a connection is given by a projection operator as in (3.2.5): $\widehat{V} : TE \to TE$, onto the vertical subspace, $V \subset TE$.

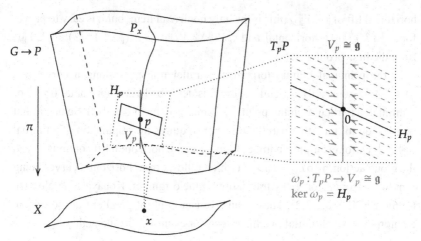

Figure 2 The relation between the Ehresmann connection form ω and a vertical projection, on the principal fiber bundle with structure group G. Taken from Wikipedia, under Creative Commons License.

operator) on differential forms, ι, so that the contraction of $\iota_{\xi^\#(\pi(p))}\Lambda$ is C^∞-linear in $\xi^\#(x)$, for any form Λ. Thus:

$$\iota_{\xi^\#(x)}\mathrm{d}\omega_p = [\omega_p, \xi(x)_p] \qquad (3.2.9)$$

Now, I will merely state Cartan's Magic Formula, describing the relation between the Lie derivative and inner and exterior derivative (which is proven inductively)

$$\mathcal{L}_{\xi^\#(x)}(\bullet) = (\iota_{\xi^\#(x)}\mathrm{d} + \mathrm{d}\iota_{\xi^\#(x)})(\bullet). \qquad (3.2.10)$$

This equation is extremely useful in differential calculus, and here it can be used to compute:

$$\mathcal{L}_{\xi^\#(x)}\omega = \iota_{\xi^\#(x)}\mathrm{d}\omega + \mathrm{d}(\omega(\xi^\#(x))) = [\omega, \xi(x)] + \mathrm{d}\xi(x), \qquad (3.2.11)$$

where, reinstating the $\pi(p)$ in place of x, we read the action of the second term on $Z \in \Gamma(TP)$ as $\mathrm{d}\xi(\pi(p))(Z) = \pi_*(Z)[\xi(\pi(p))]$, which, in a local trivialization takes the derivative of the spacetime function and leaves the Lie-algebra values intact. Equation (3.2.11) will be useful to compute the change of the connection under a change of gauge.

Let us pause here for a second to describe an important related notion, of *horizontal lift*. The horizontal lift of a vector $X_x \in T_xM$ through $p \in \pi^{-1}(x) \subset P$ is a horizontal vector X_p^h such that $\pi_*X_p^h = X_x$.

Let $[\![\bullet, \bullet]\!]_N$ be the commutator of vector fields on a smooth manifold N. Then it is easy to show that (see Kobayashi & Nomizu (1963, Prop 1.3): (i) the lift of $X + Y$ is $X^h + Y^h$, (ii) $f^h X^h$ is the lift of fX, where $f^h := f \circ \pi$, (iii) $\widehat{H}([\![X^h, Y^h]\!])$ is the horizontal lift of $[\![X,Y]\!]_M$ (this is the only nontrivial item, but it is easy to prove: for $\widehat{H}([\![X^h,Y^h]\!]_P)$ is horizontal, and $\pi_*\widehat{H}([\![X^h,Y^h]\!]_P) = \pi_*([\![X^h,Y^h]\!]_P) = [\![X,Y]\!]_M$ from the first two items.

In the principal bundle formalism parallel transport along a curve γ : $[0,1] \to M$, with $\gamma(0) = x$ and $\gamma(1) = y$, is described via a horizontal lift γ^h of γ through a particular initial point, or frame, $\gamma^h(0) = p \in \pi^{-1}(x)$. So one might be inclined to think that parallel transport requires the stipulation of an initial $p \in \pi^{-1}(x)$, for example, an initial frame. But the horizontal lift commutes with the group action, $\gamma^h \circ L_g = L_g \circ \gamma^h$ (which follows from horizontal curves being sent to horizontal curves by translation of the origin; cf. Kobayashi & Nomizu (1963, Ch. II Prop. 3.2). That means we can think of parallel transport as an isomorphism of an initial to a final fiber, for example, for the path γ:

$$\tau_\gamma : \pi^{-1}(x) \to \pi^{-1}(y). \tag{3.2.12}$$

Given two different curves, γ, γ', both between x and y, it follows that there exists a $g \in G$ such that $\tau_\gamma = g \cdot \tau_{\gamma'}$. By the composition properties of parallel transport, it is customary to focus only on closed curves γ, starting (and ending) at $x \in M$. For a path-connected M, the subgroup generated by such elements for all such closed paths depends on the base point x, only up to conjugation in G. So usually, the total group generated by parallel transport around closed curves is called *the holonomy group*, denoted by $\mathrm{Hol}(\omega)$.

It is clear that, since parallel transport can be thought of at the level of entire fibers, as in (3.2.12), there is a frame-independent abstract mathematical object that corresponds to the Ehresmann connection form, sometimes called *the Atyiah-Lie* connection. This is a section of the vector bundle T^*P/G.[26] In other words, if we know what parallel transport is at p, we know what it is at $g \cdot p$. By getting rid of this redundancy, we can find a global spacetime representation of the connection ω. This Atyiah-Lie connection is a section on the *bundle of connections*, that is, $\Upsilon \in \Gamma(T^*P/G)$, where T^*P/G is a vector bundle over spacetime.[27]

---

[26] This is defined in much the same way as the associated bundle is defined from a vector space and a principal bundle. Here I will proceed for left-invariant vector fields (i.e. those such that $L_{g*}Z = Z$), but the analogous idea works for pseudo-tensorial forms. Thus

$$(p, Z_p) \sim (g \cdot p, L_{g*}(Z_p)), \quad \text{for all} \quad g \in G. \tag{3.2.13}$$

Since locally (i.e. given some trivialization of the tangent bundle) for $x = \pi(p)$ and $\xi \in \mathfrak{g}$, we can represent $p = (x, g) := g \cdot \sigma(x)$ and $Z_p = (X_x, \xi) := \xi + \sigma_*(X_x)$, where $X_x \in T_xM$, we have, locally, $(p, v_p) = (x, g, X_x, \xi)$. If we take the quotient, we obtain that the elements of the new vector bundle will be locally of the form (x, X_x, ξ), as was to be expected from a Lie-algebra valued 1-form (or vector field).

[27] See e.g. Ciambelli & Leigh (2021, Sec. 3.2); de León & Zajac (2020, p. 9); Sardanashvily (2009, p. 60); Kolar et al. (1993, Ch. 17.4) and Gomes (2024a); Jacobs (2023) for conceptual

The Curvature

To define *curvature*, we note that an infinitesimally small parallelogram with horizontal sides that projects onto a closed parallelogram on M, may not close on P: if a horizontal parallelogram starts at $p \in P$, it may end at $g \cdot p$. In other words, the horizontal distributions need not be involutive.

Definition 5 (The curvature Ω of ω) *is a Lie-algebra valued two-form on P:*

$$\Omega(\bullet, \bullet) := \omega([\![\widehat{H}(\bullet), \widehat{H}(\bullet)]\!]_P) \tag{3.2.14}$$

Let $P(M, G)$ be a principal fiber bundle and ρ a representation of G on a finite-dimensional vector space V; $\rho(a)$ is a linear transformation of V for each $a \in G$ and $\rho(ab) = \rho(a)\rho(b)$ for $a, b \in G$. And let $\Lambda^n(N)$ be the space of alternating n-forms on a smooth manifold N.

Definition 6 (Pseudo-tensorial and tensorial forms.) *A pseudotensorial form of degree r on P of type (ρ, V) is a V-valued r-form φ on P such that*

$$L_g^* \varphi = \rho(g) \cdot \varphi \quad \text{for} \quad g \in G. \tag{3.2.15}$$

Such a form φ is called a tensorial form if it is horizontal, that is, $\varphi(X_1, \ldots, X_r) = 0$ whenever at least one of the tangent vectors X_i of P is vertical, that is, tangent to a fiber.

In other words, a pseudo-tensorial form is covariant under the group action, but not necessarily horizontal: it is only when it is also horizontal that we call it tensorial.

Then we define

Definition 7 (The *gauge covariant exterior derivative*) *of pseudo-tensorial forms as:*

$$D\varphi := (d\varphi) \circ \widehat{H}. \tag{3.2.16}$$

It is easy to show that, whereas $d\varphi$ is still only pseudo-tensorial, $D\varphi$ is tensorial, and not only pseudo-tensorial. In the language of principal fiber bundles, this is why minimal coupling, $d \to D$, renders functions "coordinate-independent": they acquire trivial dependence on the vertical directions along the fiber (which represent "coordinate" or frame changes).

---

appraisals. The bundle of connections appeared almost simultaneously in Atiyah (1957) and Kobayaschi (1957). See also Kolar et al. (1993, Ch. 17.4). To avoid confusion, it is better to refer to a section of the bundle of connections, which is itself a generalization of a connection to what are known as Lie algebroids (see Mackenzie [2005]), as an Atiyah-Lie connection.

We can rewrite (3.2.16) as:

$$D\varphi(\bullet) = d\varphi(\bullet) - d\varphi(\omega(\bullet)^{\#}), \tag{3.2.17}$$

where the second term is linear in $\omega(\bullet)^{\#}$ (i.e. can be read as $\iota_{\omega(\bullet)^{\#}} d\varphi$) and can be understood as the vertical correction to the 'gradient' of φ, so that this 'gradient' stays horizontal. We have:

$$\iota_{\omega(\bullet)^{\#}} d\varphi = \rho(\omega(\bullet))\varphi. \tag{3.2.18}$$

Locally, in a trivialization of P, we write $\varphi_{|U} \in \Gamma(\Lambda^n(\pi^{-1}(U)) \otimes V)$, so $\varphi_{|U} = \varphi_i e^i$, where $\varphi_i \in \Lambda^n(\pi^{-1}(U))$ is a real-valued pseudo-tensorial n-form, and $\{e_i\}$ is a basis for V. Then $\rho(\omega)_{|U} \in \Gamma(\Lambda^n(\pi^{-1}(U)) \otimes GL(V))$ and we can write, in this basis:

$$(\rho(\omega)\varphi)_{|U} = \rho(\omega)^i_j \wedge \varphi^j e_i, \tag{3.2.19}$$

which gives the usual expression for the action of the covariant derivative in (3.2.17). This action on other Lie-algebra valued forms will usually be written just as $[\omega, \varphi]$, with the understanding that, on a trivialization, we apply the $\wedge$ to the differential forms and the Lie bracket to the Lie algebra elements.

As with ω, pseudo-tensorial forms are only required to be equivariant under the pointwise action of the group action, as in (3.2.15). Under spacetime dependent transformations, pseudo-tensorial forms are not necessarily equivariant (satisfying something like (3.2.15)). But the gauge-covariant derivative corrects for that: that is its role. In the infinitesimal case, we now prove:

Proposition 2 *For a pseudo-tensorial form φ as per Definition 6, under an infinitesimal vertical autormorphism, $\xi(x)^{\#}$, we have the equivariance property:*

$$\mathcal{L}_{\xi^{\#}(x)}D\varphi = \rho(\xi)D\varphi \tag{3.2.20}$$

We use Cartan's Magic Formula (3.2.10) and the Lie derivative of the Ehresmann connection, given in (3.2.11), in Equation (3.2.17), written as: $D\varphi = d\varphi - \rho(\omega)\varphi$. Applying $d\iota_{\xi^{\#}(x)}$ to anything horizontal, like $D\varphi$, vanishes completely, since it first linearly contracts the horizontal form with a vertical vector. Now we apply $\iota_{\xi^{\#}(x)}d$ to $D\varphi$, obtaining (first term vanishes since $dd = 0$):

$$\iota_{\xi^{\#}(x)}d(D\varphi) = -\iota_{\xi^{\#}(x)}d(\rho(\omega)\varphi) \tag{3.2.21}$$

So, first, as will be shown in Proposition 3 just below:[28]

$$-\iota_{\xi^{\#}(x)}d\omega = -\iota_{\xi^{\#}(x)}(-[\omega, \omega]) = -[\xi(x), \omega] + [\omega, \xi(x)], \tag{3.2.22}$$

---

[28] What will be shown is that the curvature satisfies $\Omega = d\omega + [\omega, \omega]$, which vanishes on vertical vectors.

and so:

$$\iota_{\xi\#}\,d(D\varphi) = \rho(-[\xi,\omega] + [\omega,\xi])\varphi - \iota_{\xi\#}(\rho(\omega)d\varphi) \tag{3.2.23}$$

$$= (-[\rho(\xi),\rho(\omega)] + [\rho(\omega),\rho(\xi)])\varphi - \rho(\xi)d\varphi$$

$$+ \rho(\omega)\rho(\xi)\varphi \tag{3.2.24}$$

$$= \rho(\xi)(d\varphi - \rho(\omega)\varphi) = \rho(\xi)D\varphi, \tag{3.2.25}$$

where in going from the first to the second line, I used (3.2.18), and $\iota_{\xi\#}\omega = \xi$, and going from the second to the third I used $[a,b] = \frac{1}{2}(ab - ba)$. $\square$

From Proposition 2, it follows that:

$$\mathcal{L}_{\xi\#(x)}\Omega = [\xi,\Omega].^{29} \tag{3.2.26}$$

Proposition 3 *The two next definitions of curvature are equivalent to* (3.2.14):

$$\Omega = D\Omega \tag{3.2.30}$$

$$\Omega = d\omega + [\omega,\omega],$$

where d *is the exterior derivative on P.*

The proof proceeds through explicit insertion of horizontal and fundamental vertical vector fields and multi-linearity. First, one writes

$$d\omega(X,Y) = X[\omega(Y)] - Y[\omega(X)] - \omega([\![X,Y]\!]_P), \tag{3.2.31}$$

the standard formula for the exterior derivative of a 1-form. (Note: this differs from the formula in some textbooks, such as in Kobayashi & Nomizu [1963], by a factor of 2 on the left-hand-side; this gives a difference of 1/2 on the second term on (3.2.31)). So for two horizontal fields X_H, Y_H, since $\omega(X_H) = 0 = [\omega(X_H),\omega(Y_H)]$, it is immediate that :

$$(d\omega) \circ \widehat{H}(X_H, Y_H) = d\omega(X^h, Y^h) = d\omega(X^h, Y^h) + [\omega(X^h),\omega(Y^h)]. \tag{3.2.32}$$

---

[29] We can find the usual expression in terms of the non-infinitesimal transformation by noticing that

$$\rho = \mathrm{ad} : \mathfrak{g} \to GL(\mathfrak{g}); \xi \mapsto [\xi,\bullet], \tag{3.2.27}$$

or $\mathrm{ad}_\xi\eta = [\xi,\eta]$, is the tangent map at the origin to

$$\mathrm{Ad} : G \to GL(\mathfrak{g}); (g,\xi) \mapsto g^{-1}\xi g \tag{3.2.28}$$

so that under an arbitrary gauge transformation

$$F \mapsto g^{-1}Fg \tag{3.2.29}$$

And using (3.2.31) it is immediate that $d\omega(X^h, Y^h) = \omega(\llbracket\widehat{H}(X^h), \widehat{H}(Y^h)\rrbracket_P)$. This is the only case which has nonvanishing curvature. Now, for two vertical fields, the only nontrivial part of the equalities is to show that:

$$d\omega(\xi^\#, \eta^\#) = -[\omega(\xi^\#), \omega(\eta^\#)].$$

We write, for $\xi, \eta \in \mathfrak{g}$, $X = \xi^\#$, $Y = \eta^\#$, and note that, because the orbits form integral submanifolds, commutators of vertical vector fields are vertical, and $[\xi, \eta]^\# = \llbracket\xi^\#, \eta^\#\rrbracket_P$. So it follows from (3.2.31) that $d\omega(\xi^\#, \eta^\#) = -[\xi, \eta]$. I will only sketch the case for one vertical and one horizontal field (cf. Kobayashi & Nomizu (1963, Theo. 5.2) for more detail). The idea is to show that the commutator $\llbracket\xi^\#, X^h\rrbracket_P$ between a fundamental vector field $\xi^\#$ and a horizontal vector field X^h (that is covariant under G) is horizontal as well. To show that, we define the horizontal field $X^h_{g \cdot p} = L_{g*}X^h_p$, and note that the Lie derivative $\mathcal{L}_{\xi^\#}X^h = \lim_{t \to 0} \frac{1}{t}(X^h - L_{\exp(t\xi)*}X_h)$ is also horizontal, since it is the difference between two horizontal vectors at p, and so this ensures that the right-hand side of (3.2.31) vanishes. $\square$

Proposition 4 (the Bianchi identity) $D\Omega = 0$ – *this is called the Bianchi identity.*

By the definition, it is sufficient to compute its value on three horizontal vectors (the others vanish). The gauge-covariant exterior derivative is (anti)linear, so $\widehat{H}(X^h, Y^h, Z^h) = (X^h, Y^h, Z^h)$ and:

$$D\Omega(X^h, Y^h, Z^h) = (d\Omega)(X^h, Y^h, Z^h) = (dd\omega + [d\omega, \omega] - [\omega, d\omega])(X^h, Y^h, Z^h) = 0,$$
$$(3.2.33)$$

since every term has at least one contraction of ω with a horizontal vector. The Bianchi identity is a nontrivial condition that any curvature satisfies (see Baez & Munian (1994, p. 278) for the geometric interpretation of this identity). $\square$

In order to connect the definitions previously to the usual definition of Ω in terms of the exterior product, we pick out a basis for the Lie-algebra, $\{\epsilon_I \in \mathfrak{g}\}$, with structure constants c^I_{JK} defined by $\epsilon_i c^I_{JK} = [\epsilon_J, \epsilon_K]$. In terms of this basis, we write $\omega = \omega^I \epsilon_i$ and (3.2.30) becomes:

$$\Omega^I = d\omega^I - c^I_{JK}\omega^J \wedge \omega^K. \tag{3.2.34}$$

Local Sections

Locally over M, it is possible to choose a smooth embedding σ of the group identity into the fibers of P. These are called

Definition 8 (Local sections of P) *are maps* $\sigma : U \to P$ *such that* $\pi \circ \sigma =$ id.

So for $U \subset M$, there is a map $\sigma : U \to P$ such that P is locally of the form $U \times G$. For principal bundles, this need not be assumed, but follows from the definitions.

Proposition 5 (Local product structure) *Any principal bundle P, admits local diffeomorphisms* $\overline{\sigma} : U \times G \to \pi^{-1}(U)$.

Here I will only sketch the proof. The idea is to build a tubular neighborhood (see e.g. Guillemin & Pollack (2010)) around any given orbit. Roughly, we first construct a G-invariant Riemannian metric on P. In more detail, any differentiable manifold admits a Riemannian metric, and if the group G is connected and compact, we can take a smearing – an integral over the group action, using the Haar measure – of the original metric. Now one finds the orthogonal space to the orbit, at a given point $p \in P$ and uses the Riemann exponential map to find a small "slice" that intersects each orbit in a neighborhood of $\pi^{-1}(x)$ only once. This gives a local diffeomorphism between a neighborhood of $(x, \text{Id}) \in U \times G$ and a neighborhood of $p \in P$. Moving the slice up and down according to the group action spans the entire "tubular" neighborhood of the orbit, giving a diffeomorphism between $\pi^{-1}(U)$ and $U \times G$. $\square$

Definition 9 (A trivializing diffeomorphism) *is a diffeomorphism* $U \times G \simeq \pi^{-1}(U)$, *given by* $\overline{\sigma} : U \times G \to P$

The trivializing diffeomorphism is defined by a section σ:

$$\overline{\sigma} : (x, g) \mapsto g \cdot \sigma(x), \quad \text{whose inverse is} \quad \overline{\sigma}^{-1} : p \mapsto (\pi(p), g_\sigma(p)^{-1})$$

$$(3.2.35)$$

where $g_\sigma : \pi^{-1}(U) \to G$ gives $g_\sigma(p)$ as the unique group element taking p to the local section, that is, $g_\sigma(p)$ is the group element such that

$$g_\sigma(p) \cdot p = \sigma(\pi(p)).^{[30]}$$

$$(3.2.36)$$

Thus we have a condition:

$$g_\sigma(g \cdot p) = g_\sigma(p)g^{-1}.$$

$$(3.2.37)$$

Call this *equivariance* of g_σ between the given action of G on P and G's action on itself.

A transition between the trivializing diffeomorphisms $\overline{\sigma}$ and $\overline{\tau}$ takes an (x, g) in the domain of $\overline{\sigma}$ to an element in $U \times G$ in the domain of $\overline{\tau}$ by first taking $(x, g) \mapsto p = g \cdot \sigma(x)$ and then using the inverse $p \mapsto (\pi(p), g_\tau(p)^{-1})$. Since

---

[30] The precise form of g_σ will, of course, depend on σ.

$$\tau(x) = g_\tau(\sigma(x)) \cdot \sigma(x) = g_\tau(g_\sigma(p) \cdot p) \cdot (\sigma(x)) = g_\tau(p)g_\sigma^{-1}(p) \cdot \sigma(x), \quad (3.2.38)$$

it is clear that $g_\tau(p)g_\sigma^{-1}(p)$ will give the transition between the two sections. From (3.2.37):

$$g_\tau(g \cdot p)g_\sigma^{-1}(g \cdot p) = g_\tau(p)g_\sigma^{-1}(p), \quad (3.2.39)$$

so that the map $g_\tau g_\sigma^{-1}$ depends only on the fiber $\pi^{-1}(x)$, that is, depends only on $x \in M$. We call

$$g_{\tau\sigma} := g_\tau g_\sigma^{-1} : U \to G, \text{ the transition function between } \sigma \text{ and } \tau. \quad (3.2.40)$$

Thus we get a local diffeomorphism from one trivialization to another:

$$\overline{\tau}^{-1} \circ \overline{\sigma} : (x, g) \mapsto (x, gg_{\tau\sigma}). \quad (3.2.41)$$

From (3.2.40) is straightforward to see that the transition functions obey:

$$g_{\tau\sigma}g_{\sigma\tau} = \text{Id} \quad (3.2.42)$$

$$g_{\beta\tau}g_{\tau\sigma} = g_{\beta\sigma}; \quad (3.2.43)$$

which are called the cocycle conditions.

Although I will not show it here, given an atlas of charts $U_\alpha \subset M$, and local sections σ^α, we can define a principal bundle directly from the stitching together of local trivializations with transitions obeying the cocycle conditions (3.2.43); and a given P with group G is reducible to a P' with group $G' \subset G$, iff the transition functions lie in G' (see Kobayashi & Nomizu (1963, Props. 5.2 and 5.3)).

The Gauge Potentials

Given local sections σ on each chart domain U, we define a local spacetime representative of ω, as the pullback of the connection, $A^\sigma := \sigma^*\omega \in \Gamma(\Lambda^1(U) \otimes \mathfrak{g})$; (here σ is *not* a spacetime index; we momentarily keep it in the notation as a reminder of the reliance on a choice of section). In coordinates x^μ on $U \subset M$, and for $\epsilon_I \in \mathfrak{g}$ a Lie-algebra basis we write: $\sigma^*\omega = A = A_\mu^I \, dx^\mu \epsilon_I$, and $A_\mu^I \in C^\infty(U)$. Similarly, we can define the field-strength $F^\sigma = \sigma^*\Omega$. It is important to note that the sections σ are not usually horizontal: indeed, from (3.2.14) the horizontal distribution is involutive – and thus is the tangent to a submanifold of P – iff the curvature vanishes. This is why, even though the connection-form ω vanishes along horizontal directions, there is in general no section for which the pull-back A^σ vanishes: it will vanish only for a fully horizontal section.

Proposition 6 *We can use an infinitesimal transformation (as given in Equation (3.2.40)), obtaining an infinitesimally different section from a Lie-algebra* *valued function* $\xi := \xi^I \epsilon_I : U \to \mathfrak{g}$, *with coefficients* $\xi^I \in C^\infty(U)$. *The infinitesimally different representative of* ω, *already given in* (2.2.7), *is:*

$$\delta_\xi A := \mathrm{d}\xi + [A, \xi] = \mathrm{D}\xi, \quad \text{in coordinates:} \quad \delta_\xi A_\mu^I := \partial_\mu \xi^I + [A_\mu, \xi]^I = \mathrm{D}_\mu \xi^I,$$
$$(3.2.44)$$

where $\mathrm{D}_\mu(\bullet) = \partial_\mu(\bullet) + [A_\mu, \bullet]$, *the gauge-covariant derivative defined in* (3.2.17), *here acts on Lie-algebra valued scalar functions.*[31]

The proposition follows immediately from applying the pull back by σ to the Lie derivative of ω along a vertical direction, given in Equation (3.2.11). $\square$

Similarly, for $F^\sigma = \sigma^*\Omega$ (omitting the subscript σ):

$$F = \mathrm{d}A - [A, A], \quad \text{in coordinates:} \quad F_{\mu\nu}^I = \partial_{[\mu} A_{\nu]}^I - [A_\mu, A_\nu]^I, \quad (3.2.45)$$

with the square bracket in the subscripts denoting anti-symmetrization, where ∇_μ is the Levi-Civita covariant derivative on spacetime. Applying to (3.2.26) the same reasoning used to show that the gauge connection transforms as (3.2.44), we show that

$$\delta_\xi F_{\mu\nu}^I = [\xi, F_{\mu\nu}]^I. \quad (3.2.46)$$

3.2.3 Associated Bundles

In Section 3.2.1 I said that the horizontal directions encode parallel transport in vector bundles, but I have not yet described this encoding. Again it is useful to illustrate the main ideas using the tangent bundle TM and the frame bundle, $L(TM)$. We proceed as follows: take a vector X_x at a given point $x \in M$: an element of the fiber $T_x M \simeq F = \mathbb{R}^4$, where according to a frame, $\{e_I(x)\} \in L(TM)$ we write $X_x = a^I e_I \in T_x M$ as the ordered quadruplet $(a^1, \cdots, a^4) \in \mathbb{R}^4$. Each element of $P = L(TM)$ gives a linear isomorphism from $\mathbb{R}^4$ into TM.

---

[31] Note that A only captures the content of ω in directions that lie along the section σ. But it is easy to show that, in a given trivializing diffeomorphism $\overline{\sigma}$ as in (3.2.35), writing a vector $u \in T_p P$ as the doublet (u_σ, ξ), with $u_\sigma \in T_p \mathrm{Im}(\sigma)$ and $\xi \in \mathfrak{g}$, we have $\omega(u) = A(u_\sigma) + \xi$. Moreover, one can also show that there is a unique connection ω such that the $\sigma^*\omega$ for all the different sections are related by (3.2.44). The vertical component of ω – which is dynamically inert, as per the first equation of (3.2.7) – but still dependent on u, can be seen (in a suitable interpretation of differential forms, cf. Bonora & Cotta-Ramusino (1983)) as the BRST ghosts. These ghosts are classically dynamically inert, but are still field-dependent, since in general σ arises from a gauge-fixing and so it self fields dependent. And so BRST ghosts become important quantum mechanically. This interpretation geometrically encodes quantum gauge transformations through the BRST differential (Thierry-Mieg, 1980). Although interesting in its own right, we will not explore this topic here. See Gomes (2019); Gomes & Riello (2017) for more about the relationship between ghosts and connection forms.

We can rotate the frame by a matrix g^I_J to obtain $\{g^I_J e_I(x)\} \in L(TM)$. The components of X_x will change accordingly, as $a^K \mapsto a^K g^{-1}_{KL}$. With the two transformations, we obtain the same vector: $a^K g^{-1}_{KL} g^{LI} e_I = a^I e_I$. Thus, if we write a doublet (p, v) as, respectively, the frame and the components, we want to identify (gp, vg^{-1}) (where we have simplified the notation for the action of the group to be just juxtaposition). So we get an *associated bundle*, denoted by $TM \simeq L(TM) \times_\rho \mathbb{R}^4$

$$L(TM) \times_\rho \mathbb{R}^4 = L(TM) \times \mathbb{R}^4/\sim \quad \text{where} \quad (p,v) \sim (gp, vg^{-1}), \qquad (3.2.47)$$

and denote the equivalence classes with square brackets: $[p, v] \in L(TM) \times_\rho \mathbb{R}^4$. More generally, E is a vector bundle over M with typical fiber V that is associated to P with structure group G, iff:

$$P \times_\rho F = P \times F/\sim \quad \text{where} \quad (p,v) \sim (gp, \rho(g^{-1})v), \qquad (3.2.48)$$

where $\rho : G \to GL(V)$ is a representation of G on V. Similarly as to the case with $\mathbb{R}^4$, given any vector bundle E, we could construct a principal bundle as $L(E)$, and recover $E = L(E) \times_\rho V$.

Connections on an Associated Bundle

Once we have constructed associated bundles in this way, parallel transport for any vector bundle comes naturally from a notion of horizontality in the principal bundle. To find the parallel transport of the vector X_x along Y_x, take the curve $\gamma(t) \in M$ with $\gamma(0) = x$, so that $\gamma'(0) = Y_x$. Given a frame $p_x \in P$ so that $\pi(p_x) = x$, we take the horizontal lift of $\gamma(t)$ through p_x: call it $\gamma^h(t)$. Let $X_x = [p_x, v]$, where $v \in V$ are the components of X_x in terms of the basis p_x. By definition, the curve in E given by $[\gamma^h(t), v]$ is parallel transported, that is, gives a parallel transport of X_x along $\gamma(t)$. Now, we define $v_X : P \to V$ such that, for all $p \in P$

$$X(\pi(p)) = [p, v_X(p)], \quad \text{where} \quad v_X(g \cdot p) = g^{-1}v_X(p); \qquad (3.2.49)$$

that is, $v_X(p)$ are the components of $X(\pi(p))$ on the basis p (and therefore v_X obeys the covariance property on the right of (3.2.49)). Thus we define the covariant derivative of X along Y at x, as:

$$D_Y X(x) := \left[\gamma^h(0), \frac{d}{dt}\Big|_{t=0} v_X(\gamma^h(t))\right], \qquad (3.2.50)$$

where $\frac{d}{dt}\big|_{t=0} v_X$ acts component-by-component. In words, we compare the parallel transported components of X with the actual components of X; their nonconstancy corresponds to the failure of X to be parallel transported, and

to the non-vanishing covariant derivative of X. In this way a covariant derivative is just the standard derivative of the vector components as described in the
horizontal – or parallel transported – frame.

In practice, this definition is employed by choosing a particular trivialization,
or basis of frames on an open set $U \subset M$ for an associated vector bundle E, with
typical fiber V; this is a section of the bundle of frames $L(E)$. Call this basis
$\sigma = \{e_i\}_{i=1}^k$ and its algebraic dual $\sigma^* = \{e^i\}_{i=1}^k$. A linear transformation of E_x
is an element of $\text{End}(E_x) := E_x^* \otimes E_x$, and we can describe the extent to which
the chosen basis is nonparallel along a certain direction by a 1-form valued on
such linear transformations, which we write as:

$$\omega^\sigma = \omega^{\sigma j}{}_i \otimes e^i \otimes e_j \in \Gamma(T^*U \otimes (E \otimes E^*)) \tag{3.2.51}$$

where $\omega^{\sigma j}{}_i \in \Gamma(T^*U)$. Thus, for $X \in (T_xM)$,

$$D_X e_j = \omega^{\sigma i}{}_j(X)e_i. \tag{3.2.52}$$

Now for some section of the real (or complex) vector bundle $s \in \Gamma(E)$, we
locally write $s = s^i e_i$, and the covariant derivative of s becomes:

$$Ds = ds^j \otimes e_j + s^i \omega^{\sigma j}{}_i \otimes e_j. \tag{3.2.53}$$

Admissible Bases and Subgroups of GL(n)

If the principal bundle is construed as just a bundle of linear frames, how can we
justify a restriction of to a subset of the most general group of transformations
between frames? The restriction corresponds to the preservation of some added
structure to V. In other words, when V is not just a bare vector space, but, for
example, a normed vector space, we would like changes of basis to preserve this
structure, for example, the orthonormality of the basis vectors, and this restricts
the bundle of linear frames to the appropriate sub-bundle, of *admissible frames*.
This sub-bundle has as its structure group the automorphisms of a typical fiber
that has more than just the linear vector space structure that we started off with.

Let us illustrate the relationship between the structure of the fiber and the
set of frames that are adapted to it. Suppose that the typical fiber has an added
positive-definite inner product structure: $(\cdot, \cdot)$ as the canonical inner product in
$\mathbb{R}^4$, and $p \in P$ as a linear isomorphism from $\mathbb{R}^4$ to $T_{\pi(p)}M$. Then we can define
an inner product on TM, for $X, Y \in T_xM$ as

$$(p^{-1}X, p^{-1}Y) = \langle X, Y \rangle, \tag{3.2.54}$$

where invariance of $(\cdot, \cdot)$ by $O(n)$ implies the inner product is independent of
which basis $p \in \pi^{-1}(x)$ we take. The converse – that a Riemannian structure
$\langle \cdot, \cdot \rangle$ for the associated bundle induces a subbundle for $L(TM)$ – is also easy

to show: again, seeing $p \in P$ as a linear isomorphism from $\mathbb{R}^4$ to $T_{\pi(p)}M$, $p \in P \subset L(TM)$ iff given $u, v \in \mathbb{R}^4$ we have $(u, v) = \langle pu, pv \rangle$.[32] This corresponds to $G = O(4)$; similarly, $SO(4)$ adds an orientation to $\mathbb{R}^4$. But we can extend these constructions to more general cases, in which the typical fiber is not soldered onto spacetime. For instance, $G = U(n)$ corresponds to V being a complex n-dimensional vector space with a Hermitean inner product on; and $G = SU(n)$ adds an orientation, and so on. The moral is that the added structure on V induces an added structure on the associated vector bundle if and only if the transformation group $G \subset GL(n)$ preserves that added structure.

3.2.4 Getting Rid of Associated Bundles

Here we will look at how certain structures of E seen as an associated bundle to P (e.g. as $L(E) \times_\rho V$) can be understood directly on E, without mention of P.

Relation to Connections of E Expressed without Frames of $L(E)$

We can also describe a connection on E directly in terms of a trivialization of E, without mentioning $L(E)$ and a choice of basis therein. For that, recall the expression of the covariant derivative directly in terms of the vector bundle, as in Equation (3.2.2). Call $C(E)$ the space of covariant derivatives for E, and let: $\Delta(E) := \Gamma(T^*M \otimes \text{End}(E))$. Given any $D_o, D \in C(E)$, there exists a $\omega_D^o \in \Delta(E)$ such that $D_o - D = \omega_D^o$. Therefore the map:[33]

$$\Delta(E) \to C(E)$$
$$\omega \mapsto D_o - \omega \qquad\qquad (3.2.55)$$

is a bijection: that is, the space of covariant derivatives is an affine space over the vector space of connections, $\Delta(E)$. This is why, in any trivialization of E – a trivialization that plays the analogous role of the choice of frames of $L(E)$ in (3.2.53) – we can take $D_o \to d \otimes \text{Id}$, and take connections to parametrize the space of covariant derivatives. Ultimately, it is why the covariant derivatives are described as vector bosons: 1-forms valued on $\text{End}(E)$, a fact that will be important in Section 4.

---

[32] In more detail and generality, define $P \times_\rho V$ as the equivalence class for the doublet $(p, v) \in P \times V$ with $(p, v) \sim (g \cdot p, \rho(g^{-1})v)$. Suppose that V is a Riemannian vector space, with metric $\langle \cdot, \cdot \rangle$. We can induce a metric in $P_F = P \times_\rho V$ defining, for any p and $v, v' \in V$: $\langle [p, v], [p, v'] \rangle := \langle v, v' \rangle$. To be well-defined, we must have:

$$\langle [p, v], [p, v'] \rangle = \langle [g \cdot p, \rho(g^{-1})v], [g \cdot p, \rho(g^{-1})v'] \rangle = \langle \rho(g^{-1})v, \rho(g^{-1})v' \rangle :$$

which is true only if the action of the group on V is orthogonal with respect to the metric.

[33] I here abuse notation and use the same label for an element of $\Delta(E)$ that I used for an Ehresmann connection: there are only so many letters in all the alphabets!

Of course, under a change of frame, ω^σ given in (3.2.51) will transform in the familiar, inhomogeneous form, given in (3.2.17) (or (3.2.44)). This gives a passive interpretation of gauge transformations. But we can formulate the corresponding active interpretation in terms of $\Delta(E)$ by considering two fiber-wise linearly isomorphic vector bundles, $E, \widetilde{E}$, over M (i.e. related by a diffeomorphism $f : E \to \widetilde{E}$ such that $\pi_E \circ f = \pi_{\widetilde{E}}$, where f takes $\pi_E^{-1}(x) \to \pi_{\widetilde{E}}^{-1}(x)$ by a linear isomorphism).

Two connections, D and $\tilde{D}$, in two linearly isomorphic vector bundles are isomorphic if they are related by conjugation by the linear isomorphism. This relation guarantees that the following diagram commutes (for all $X \in \Gamma(TM)$):

$$
\begin{array}{ccc}
\Gamma(E) & \xrightarrow{D_X} & \Gamma(E) \\
f \downarrow & & \downarrow f \\
\Gamma(\widetilde{E}) & \xrightarrow[\tilde{D}_X]{} & \Gamma(\widetilde{E})
\end{array}
$$

Thus we can represent the connection D under a bundle isomorphism obtaining a new connection

$$\tilde{D}_X(s) = f D_X(f^{-1} s) \Rightarrow \tilde{D}_X = f D_X f^{-1} \tag{3.2.56}$$

or equivalently, $f D_X = \tilde{D}_X f$. And, of course, if D is related to ω and $\tilde{D}$ is related to $\tilde{\omega}$ then the relationship between ω and $\tilde{\omega}$ is that given in (3.2.11) (or (3.2.44)).[34]

The Structure Group *G* as a Holonomy Group

As with the fiber-wise application of (3.2.12), which could be seen in terms of frames, we can define parallel transport for vector bundles as a linear isomorphism between different fibers. Given a covariant derivative (3.2.2) and a curve $\gamma \in M$ such that $\gamma(0) = x$, where E is the vector bundle and E_x is the fiber over $x \in M$, we define the parallel transport along γ as a unique linear isomorphism:

$$\tau_{\gamma(t)} : E_x \to E_{\gamma(t)} \tag{3.2.58}$$

---

[34] Over $\pi_E^{-1}(U) = \pi_{\widetilde{E}}^{-1}(U)$, the domain of a trivialization, we can set $\tilde{D}_o = d$, obtaining $f D_X = \tilde{D}_X f$:

$$f D_X e_i = f \omega_i^k(X) e_k = \omega_i^k(X) f_k^j e_j = (\omega_i^l(X) f_l^k) e_k$$
$$\tilde{D}_X(f e_i) = \tilde{D}_X(f_i^j e_j) = (df_i^k + f_i^j \tilde{\omega}_j^k(X)) e_k$$
$$\therefore \quad df_i^k + f_i^j \tilde{\omega}_j^k(X) = \omega_i^l(X) f_l^k.$$

Valid for all $X \in \Gamma(TM_{|U})$. We then obtain:

$$\tilde{\omega} = (df) f^{-1} + f \omega f^{-1} \tag{3.2.57}$$

such that given any $X_x \in E_x$,

$$D_{\gamma'}(\tau_{\gamma(t)}(X_x)) = 0, \tag{3.2.59}$$

where $\tau_{\gamma(t)}(X_x) \in \Gamma(E|_{\gamma})$. or $\gamma, \gamma' : [0, 1] \to M$, with $\gamma(0) = \gamma'(0)$ and $\gamma(1) = \gamma'(1) = y$:

$$g \cdot \tau_{\gamma} = \tau_{\gamma'}, \quad !g \in \mathsf{End}(E_y), \tag{3.2.60}$$

If the covariant derivative preserves the structure on the typical fiber (so would correspond to an Ehresmann connection on the bundle of admissible frames, as described next), then in (3.2.60) we have $g \in \mathsf{Aut}(E_y) \subset \mathsf{End}(E_y)$, where $\mathsf{Aut}(E_y)$ is the group of linear automorphisms that are not only linear (so not only in $\mathsf{End}(E_y)$) but that preserve the added structure on E_y. Alternatively, by the composition properties of parallel transport, we can see parallel transport around a closed curve starting (and ending) at $x \in M$ as an element $g \in \mathsf{Aut}(E_x)$. If we take all the closed curves, this generates a subgroup of $\mathsf{Aut}(E_x)$ called $\mathsf{Hol}_{(x)}(D)$.

It can be shown that, on a simply-connected region, the holonomy depends on x only up to conjugation by a group element. Thus it is customary to refer to the path-independent $\mathsf{Hol}(D)$ as *the holonomy group* $\mathsf{Hol}(D)$. From "Relation to Connections of E Expressed without Frames of $L(E)$" section, it follows that, for two linearly isomorphic bundles, $E, \widetilde{E}$, $\mathsf{Hol}(D) = \mathsf{Hol}(\widetilde{D})$. It can also be shown that, given a connection D, one can find a principal bundle (P, M, G), with a connection ω, such that the holonomy group is isomorphic (as a G-torsor) to the structure group G, and E is an associated bundle to P with D being the induced connection from ω (cf. Michor (2008, Theo. 17.11)).

3.3 Summary of Classical Gauge Theory

We are now in place to summarize the basic ingredients for the classical description of the interaction between a particle and a gauge field, whose elements we have surveyed thus far. To do so we need to employ both associated vector bundles, principal fiber bundles and Ehresmann connections. Different matter fields are represented as sections of different vector bundles. These fields interact via different forces of nature, with each force being associated to a Lie group. By associating a collection of vector bundles with the same principal bundle, we ensure that the parallel transports of a collection of matter fields that are charged under the same force are coordinated. For example, charged scalar, electron, and quark-fields all interact electromagnetically; and that interaction is mediated by the same fundamental electromagnetic field (*mutatis mutandis*, for other interactions, e.g., replacing "electromagnetism" by the "strong force"). This means that the relevant covariant derivative operators on the vector bundles in which these matter fields are valued have the same parallel transport properties.

So here are the basic ingredients of a gauge theory of particles:

1. **A smooth (semi) Riemannian manifold** M. – This plays the role of spacetime.

2. **A finite-dimensional vector space** F **equipped with an inner product** $\langle \cdot, \cdot \rangle$. - This is the space where the field corresponding to a particle takes its values. This space is determined by the internal structure of the particle in question (phase, isospin, etc.) and is called the internal space. Typical examples are $\mathbb{C}, \mathbb{C}^2, \mathbb{C}^4$ or (in the standard interpretation; not in that of Section 4) Lie algebras $\mathfrak{u}(1), \mathfrak{su}(2)$.

3. **A Lie group** G **and a representation** $\rho : G \to GL(V)$ **orthogonal with respect to** $\langle \cdot, \cdot \rangle$. - G then acts on the bases of internal states at each point. The orthogonality of the representation is necessary for the inner product not to depend on the chosen basis of internal states.

4. **A principal** G-**bundle over** M: (P, π, M, G). - This bundle can be identified with the bundle of admissible G-bases over M. A section of P is an admissible G-reference relative to which we describe, for example, our wave function.

5. **A connection** ω **on** P, **with curvature** Ω. - This connection provides us with the intrinsic variation of bases. Applied over a local reference s, we obtain the **local gauge potential**, $A = \sigma^*\omega$. Similarly, we obtain the **local curvature**, $F = \sigma^*\Omega$. Thus far, all of the previous items have described non-dynamical features of the models; that is, not subject to a gauge variational principle; this is the first dynamical element of the theory.

6. **A global section** φ **of the associated vector bundle** $P \times_\rho F$. - Matter fields will be associated with such sections that satisfy the Euler-Lagrange equations of some action functional involving the local potentials A.

7. **An action** $S(\Phi, \omega)$ **whose stationary points are classical solutions.** - Typically, this functional is of the form:

$$S(\varphi, \omega) = a \int_M \|\Omega\|^2 + c\|D\varphi\|^2 \tag{3.3.1}$$

where D is the covariant exterior derivative determined by ω, which ensures, together with the norm on the algebra and tensor fields $\| \bullet \|$, that the action functional is gauge invariant. The constant a is called the *normalization constant*, and c is the *coupling constant*.

In the next section, we will see how these ingredients come together in models of particle physics.

4 Why Gauge? A Geometrical Reason

In Section 3 we saw one sense in which gauge theory is geometrical, and here we will look at another. Clearly, the label "geometrical" is ambiguous. For instance, it is often taken to connote properties related to distance relations. Although there is one interpretation of gauge theories and gauge transformations that is geometric in this sense – called Kaluza-Klein theory – that is also not the sense we will focus on here. Here I want to assess whether gauge transformations can be understood naturally as automorphisms of a local and internal geometric structure, like Lorentz transformations are automorphisms of the local Lorentzian metric; and whether the Ehresmann connection can be understood as determining parallel transport for this internal geometry, like an affine connection determines parallelism for tensor fields over spacetime.

In this enterprise we encounter two putative disanalogies: one minor and one major. In brief, the minor putative disanalogy between local gauge symmetries and local spacetime symmetries is that, apparently, the Ehresmann connection makes ineliminable use of principal fiber bundles, whereas the Levi-Civita connection for spacetime does not. However, as I presaged in Section 3.2.1 (cf. discussion after Equation (3.2.2)), this minor disanalogy is a consequence of the fact that for spacetimes we only use tensor bundles over TM, whereas we seem to need unrelated vector bundles for gauge theory. This fact leads to the major putative disanalogy: in the gauge case we stipulate by hand that different vector bundles are associated to the same principal bundle, which is why they covary under parallel transport, whereas in the spacetime case different tensor bundles obligatorily covary under parallel transport. In Section 4.1 I will describe this major putative disanalogy in more detail. Then, in Section 4.2, I will describe the minor putative disanalogy and already dispel it by recalling aspects of Section 3.2.4. In Section 4.3 I will dispel the major putative disanalogy: a more laborious enterprise, that will involve showing that the whole content of the SM consists of fields living on certain internal spaces.

And here is this section's answer to these putative disanalogies, in slogan form: gauge transformations can be understood naturally as automorphisms of an internal geometric structure, to which the theory is ontologically committed; and the Ehresmann connection can be understood as defining parallel transport in these spaces, similarly to the Levi-Civita connection determining parallelism for tensor fields over spacetime.

4.1 A Major Putative Disanalogy between Gauge Theory and Gravity

In their modern mathematical guise, particles exist as sections of distinct vector bundles over spacetime. In more colloquial terms, particles are described by fields that take values in a variety of internal vector spaces coexisting over each spacetime point. In the standard mathematical explanation that we saw in Section 3.2.2, those fields that interact are associated to a single principal G-bundle, P – where G is the symmetry group regimenting a particular interaction – and each principal bundle is endowed with a single Ehresmann affine connection ω. Thus, in the Standard Model of particle physics (SM henceforth), all fields charged under the same gauge group get their parallel transport from the same mathematical object, ω; that is why their parallel transport "marches in step." In the words of Weatherall (2016, p. 2401):

> Principal bundles are auxiliary [in the sense that only] vector bundles represent possible local states of matter; principal bundles coordinate between these vector bundles ... [they are auxiliary] in the sense in which a coach is auxiliary to the players on the field.

This is a beguiling metaphor, but is it explanatory? It certainly falls short of the familiar geometric explanation for symmetry and parallel transport that we get in general relativity. There, all tensor fields co-rotate under parallel transport because they are sections of vector bundles built from the same tangent bundle, *TM*. It is the tangent bundle that underpins a unified account of parallel transport for tensor fields.

In the gauge case, the textbook tradition – indeed, so far as I know, the extant literature[35] – reveals no similarly powerful explanation for why the fields that couple through the strong force march in step under parallel transport.

Of course, there is a straightforward definition of covariant derivative for an arbitrary vector bundle (given in Equation (3.2.2)) that specializes, when the vector bundle is the tangent bundle, to the usual definition of covariant derivatives. This definition does not mention frames, groups, and so on. So there is no disanalogy there. But that formulation of covariant derivative is "bundle-solipsist": it works for each matter field but offers us no link between fields. Using this covariant derivative leaves the "marching-in-step" of sections of any two different vector bundles under parallel transport *completely* mysterious.

Thus a halfway house to solving this "coordination problem" is the textbook's demand that particles whose parallel transport should march in step are

---

[35] I thank Lathan Boyle and David Tong for helpful discussions of this curious lacuna in the literature.

all associated to the same principal fiber bundle, with the same structure group
and Ehresmann connection. This is only a halfway house because, in Weatherall's vivid metaphor, in the textbook tradition we *choose* to assign a single coach
to all of the players.

To summarize, here is the major putative disanalogy that we are addressing in
this section: it is clear why in general relativity the same Levi-Civita connection
should guide the parallel transport of different tensor fields; it is clear why they
co-rotate or march in step. Whereas it is *not* yet clear why the same Ehresmann
connection should guide the parallel transport of different gauge fields.

4.2 Parallel Transport and Frame Dependence

Here is a minor putative disanalogy, that we should get out of the way. Lie
groups seem to appear *explicitly* in the principal fiber bundles encoding the
parallel transport of particles field, whereas these groups need not be invoked
for the parallel transport of tensor fields in spacetime.

The formulation of general relativity that is most apt to expound the two putative disanalogies employs an orthonormal basis of vectors at each spacetime
point and a connection-form that describes their parallel transport.

The different orthonormal bases are related by elements of the Lie group
$O(3, 1)$ (or $SO(3, 1)$, if spacetime orientation is important). But this is also the
group that leaves the Minkowski metric on a $3 + 1$ space invariant (and its subgroup of orientation preserving transformations). In other words, the symmetry
group – for example, $SO(3, 1)$ – that acts on the orthonormal bases is tied to the
preservation of the structure of a 'typical fiber'; so $SO(3, 1) \simeq \text{Aut}(T_x M)$, with
only the particular isomorphism being given by a choice of frame. Thus, in general relativity, the reason we obtain an $SO(3, 1)$ action on the space of frames
is that each fiber $T_x M$ has a Lorentzian inner product structure.

Similarly, as we saw in Section 3.2.3, Lie groups of a principal bundle seen as
a bundle of frames of a vector bundle reflect the structure of the vector bundle's
typical fiber in a frame independent way: the gauge group is no longer postulated as fundamental but instead acquires meaning as the invariance group of
the typical fiber of E. Moreover, as we saw in "The Structure Group G as a
Holonomy Group" section, we can think of parallel transport on a vector bundle in a frame-independent way as being a structure preserving map, carrying
the fiber's structure from one point of spacetime to another along a spacetime
path (cf. Equation (3.2.60)). Differences in parallel transport give rise to the
holonomy group, which recovers the gauge group G (as the group of automorphisms of the typical fiber). Just as well, they recover in this manner the group
$SO(3, 1)$ in the case of spacetime.

In sum, for both spacetime tensors and vector bundles, covariant derivatives can be characterized invariantly, without mentioning frames, gauges, and so on. In the same way we think of the Levi-Civita connection as determining the rotation of the local tangent space as one moves from one point to another (and not as the explicit transport of a specific tangent basis), we think of an affine connection on a vector bundle as determining the rotation of internal spaces.

4.3 How to Dispel the Putative Disanalogy: The Internal Spaces

This section will dispel the second putative disanalogy between parallel transport of spacetime and internal quantities. And here is the compulsory warning: this section's approach to gauge theory is idiosyncratic; it is not part of the standard lore about gauge theory and so the Section gets a #.

Let us first set aside all questions about the 'external' spacetime geometry. A matter field can be described as the tensor product between an "internal" and an "external" component: the internal space – for example, $\mathbb{C}^2$ – on which gauge fields take values, and external spinor fields in the case of matter fields, or external tensor fields X in the case of gauge bosons. So, in the standard formulation, gauge fields are acted on by representations of the gauge group and its Lie algebra, while, for example, spinor fields are acted on by representations of the Spin group and its Lie algebra ($\mathfrak{so}(3, 1)$), which correspond to changes of frames for the tangent bundle. Here, I will focus only on the gauge part.

Now, in order to interpret the Ehresmann connection and gauge transformations as on a par with the Levi-Civita connection we need to respond to the major putative disanalogy: in the SM, different fields live in different spaces, and the Ehresmann connection lives outside of these spaces but plays an auxiliary role. Here we will see that interacting fields can be seen as sections of bundles built up from the same internal spaces, or typical fibers. For instance, in the same way that a symmetric, covariant tensor of rank two is built from two copies of TM, (the internal part of) quarks will have components in a typical fiber isomorphic to $\mathbb{C}^3$, and gluons will be certain (symmetrized, traceless) tensor bundles, involving $\mathbb{C}^3$ and $\mathbb{C}^{*3}$. Thus, by describing the connection form ω in the bundle of admissible frames of $(E, M, \mathbb{C}^3)$, we have a geometric reason for the parallel transport of the different quarks and leptons marching in step. This allows us to understand a principal bundle P, not as "fundamental and yet auxiliary," but as a bundle of frames of a *single* vector bundle E for each force, which is what figures in our ontology. This argument will, of course, require a brief description of the particle content of the SM.

The SM is represented in terms of Weyl fermions, which are two-component spacetime spinors. But I am only interested in the structure of the internal spaces; the spaces where the gauge connections act. So here I am basically ignoring the spacetime spinor structure of the SM (though they are somewhat implicit in the notation of left- or right-handed particles to be used subsequently). When representing the full fermionic content of the SM, this spinor part would be included as factors in a tensor product with the internal part that I am interested in and aim to describe in this section. I will get back to this point next.

The part of the (minimal) SM that I am interested in consists of forty-five complex numbers, organized into three generations, which means it has the same structure repeated three times. We can understand this repetition in terms of direct sums:

$$\mathbb{C}^{45} = \mathbb{C}^{15} \oplus \mathbb{C}^{15} \oplus \mathbb{C}^{15} \tag{4.3.1}$$

The following table tells us how these components transform, and it is organized into blocks whose elements can transform into each other (elements from different generations, or blocks, cannot). So each $\mathbb{C}^{15}$ breaks down into the five rows of the following table (I will here only focus on the first generation).[36]

Now let us unpack Table 1. First, the columns are labeled with the groups that are associated to the types of interaction: strong ($SU(3)$), weak ($SU(2)$), and hyperweak ($U(1)$).

- **The quarks:** are represented by the first three rows of the table. As to the first column: quarks clearly feel the strong forces, and they transform under the

Table 1 The representation of the SM groups on fermions.

	$SU(3)$	$SU(2)$	$U(1)$
q_L	3	2	$\frac{1}{6}$
u_R	3	1	$\frac{2}{3}$
d_R	3	1	$-\frac{1}{3}$
ℓ_L	1	2	$-\frac{1}{2}$
e_R	1	1	-1

---

[36] The three generations differ mostly with respect to their Yukawa couplings to the Higgs, which I am ignoring here. These are nongauge interactions that lead to different masses of the three generations. Also note that here I am describing the *minimal* SM, and so I am not including the right-handed neutrinos, which have not yet been directly observed, but, after the discovery of neutrino oscillations, are generally assumed to exist.

standard, or fundamental, representation of $SU(3)$, labeled "3," which just means $SU(3)$ acts on elements of $\mathbb{C}^3$ via matrices which preserve the volume element and complex inner product of $\mathbb{C}^3$. So the components of quarks corresponding to the first row can be seen as vectors in internal spaces isomorphic to (a structured) $\mathbb{C}^3$. Now, q_L is a left-handed quark doublet, which is a doublet of the form $q_L = (u_L, d_L)$. In the first generation this would be called up-left and down-left, respectively; in the second generation it would be charm-left and strange-left, and in the third generation it would be top-left and bottom left. The reason q_L is called a doublet – unlike the two rows beneath it, representing the up-right and the down-right quarks, u_R and d_R which are singlets – is that the components of q_L, namely, u_L and d_L, are charged under the weak nuclear force, and transform into each other under the action of $SU(2)$. In the entry corresponding to $q_L \times SU(2)$ this transformation property is represented by the number 2, which means that q_L transforms as an element of $\mathbb{C}^2$ under the fundamental representation of $SU(2)$. The number 1 for the entries $u_R \times SU(2)$ and $d_R \times SU(2)$ means that u_R and d_R are neutral under the weak forces, so cannot transform into each other (because, being singlets, they don't transform at all under $SU(2)$). Finally, the left-handed quark has a "weak hypercharge" of $-1/6$ under $U(1)$, which means that it is a complex number (an element of $\mathbb{C}$) which under the action of a given $U(1)$ phase shift generator ξ, has its phase rotate at the rate of $-\xi/6$ (or $e^{i\xi/6}$); *mutatis mutandis* for the down-right and up-right quarks.[37]

- **The leptons:** are represented by the remaining three rows in the table and have a kind of parallel structure to the quarks, but, of course, they are all neutral under $SU(3)$ (they are not charged under strong interactions). ℓ_L is the left-handed lepton doublet, which is of the form $\ell_L = (e_L, \nu_L)$. In the first generation these are the left-handed electron and neutrino (in the second and third they get "muon" and "tau" prefixes). Again, we put e_L and ν_L in the same row because they are charged under $SU(2)$ (they are charged under the weak forces), and transform into each other, unlike the particle of the remaining row – the right-handed electron e_R which is neutral under $SU(2)$. The hypercharge of ℓ_L is $-1/2$ (which does not coincide with its electric charge; see footnote 37). The electric charge of the right-handed electron, is, as expected, 1.

With the basic ingredients in place, I will now, in Section 4.3.1 defend my interpretation of Table 1, arguing that it dispels the major (putative) disanalogy between gauge and gravity that I described previously. In Section 4.3.2, I will present five possible objections to my interpretation.

---

[37] Note that for $U(1)$ it is a 0 entry – and not a 1, as it is for $SU(3)$ and $SU(2)$ – that tells us a particle does not transform, or is neutral with respect to this interaction.

4.3.1 Interpretation

The first two columns of Table 1 contain only one kind of nontrivial representation: the fundamental. So, in these columns, elements of $SU(3)$ and $SU(2)$ are 3×3 and 2×2 matrices, respectively, acting on elements of $\mathbb{C}^3$ and $\mathbb{C}^2$, preserving their canonical inner product and oriented volume.[38] The third column, under $U(1)$ is, in one sense, the most familiar from classical electromagnetism: it represents an overall phase, where different charges transform with different rotation speeds under $U(1)$.[39]

So we clearly have $\mathbb{C}^3, \mathbb{C}^2, \mathbb{C}^1$ over each spacetime point, where particles take their values. These are the typical fibers of three different fundamental vector bundles, call them $(E^3, M, \mathbb{C}^3), (E^2, M, \mathbb{C}^2), (E^1, M, \mathbb{C}^1)$, or E^3, E^2, E^1 for short, where, for each, a fiber at a point is isomorphic to a complex vector space with inner product and orientation: for $\pi_n : E^n \to M, \pi_n^{-1}(x) \simeq \mathbb{C}^n$ (but recall: there is no canonical isomorphism). Each of these vector bundles is analogous to TM in the spacetime case, and we also naturally have the dual bundles (of linear functionals): E^{3*}, E^{2*}, E^{1*}, that are necessary in order to represent the corresponding anti-particles. The group of automorphisms of these fibers are, again, (noncanonically) isomorphic to $SU(3), SU(2)$, and $U(1)$, respectively, which necessarily emerge via (3.2.60), or upon the introduction of a frame, as explained in Section 4.2.

Now, as usual, we can join these vector bundles in different ways, using different kinds of products; and as for tensor fields over spacetime, here too, the most important for our purposes is the tensor product.[40] Of course, a group action or representation on a vector space V induces a representation on arbitrary tensor products of V and V^*; and so it is here: the structure of the typical

---

[38] A special unitary matrix is a unitary transformation with determinant 1. We can interpret the restriction to determinant 1 as preserving the oriented volume because the signed n-dimensional volume of a n-dimensional parallelepiped is expressed by a determinant, and the determinant of a linear endomorphism determines how the orientation and the n-dimensional volume are transformed under the endomorphism. Alternatively, $U(n)$ is the n-fold cover of $SU(n) \times U(1)$.

[39] I should also note that weak hypercharge, denoted Y_W, is not the same as electric charge, Q. The relation between the two types of charge emerges only after symmetry breaking, which requires an interaction between the Higgs and weak isospin: it is given by the equation (in our convention) $Q = 2T_3 + Y_W$, where T is the $SU(2)$ charge, and we have assumed the Higgs potential selects the third component of isospin. It coincides with electric charge only for the rows that transform trivially under $SU(2)$, namely, for all the right-handed particles in the table. Thus, the electric charge of the down-right quark is $-1/3$, for an up-right quark it is $2/3$, and so on. The way these charges combine after symmetry-breaking gives a mnemonic device for the numbers of the last column: the entry for the left-handed particles is the average of the two entries below, for right-handed particles.

[40] Given two vector bundles $E, \bar{E}$ over the same spacetime M, the tensor bundle is a bundle over M whose fiber over $x \in M$ is $E_x \otimes \bar{E}_x$.

fiber defines a group that acts on that typical fiber, and that action naturally extends to all tensor products.[41]

In the first row the left-handed quark doublet has components lying along $\mathbb{C}^3, \mathbb{C}^2$, and $\mathbb{C}^1$: we must locate it within a space of three colors, and of two isospin charges, and of one hypercharge. The internal part of the left-handed quark doublet is a section of the bundle

$$q_L \in \Gamma(E^3 \otimes E^2 \otimes E^1). \qquad (4.3.2)$$

Unlike the first row of Table 1, the particles in the following two rows have no component along $\mathbb{C}^2$, which is why they are not charged under $SU(2)$. So for example, the down-right quark has three options for color, and only one option for isospin and electric charge. In contrast, the left-handed lepton doublet has no components along $\mathbb{C}^3$, but has components along $\mathbb{C}^2$; and the right-handed electron has no components along either $\mathbb{C}^3$ or $\mathbb{C}^2$ (that is why it is not charged under either the strong or the weak interactions) it only has components along $\mathbb{C}^1$ (cf. footnote 37).

As I said previously, the odd man out in Table 1 is the third column, corresponding to the $U(1)$ weak hypercharges, since there we have multiple non-neutral values. How should we interpret the different weak hypercharges as properties of sections of vector bundles? One immediate answer comes from a rather trivial technical point. Since $\mathbb{C}^1$ has complex dimension 1, arbitrary tensor products of $\mathbb{C}^1$ will also have complex dimension 1.[42] But if a particle is, formally, a section of a vector bundle $E^1 \otimes E^1 := E^1_2$, under a rotation of E^1's typical fiber $\mathbb{C}$ by θ, because of the multilinearity of the tensor product, that section of E^1_2 picks up a phase of 2θ. Thus, formally, taking the lowest charge as the unit, we can think of a weak hypercharge of $\frac{N}{6}$ as being due to the N-th tensor product of E^1, which we call E^1_N, and negative charges are sections of tensor products of $(E^1)^*$. But, precisely because these tensor products are still 1-dimensional, not much changes in terms of the representation of these sections: there are no added degrees of freedom.[43]

---

[41] For instance, if $\rho(g)$ is a representation of G on V, then G acts on the dual space V^* via the inverse of the transpose, $\rho(g^{-1})^T$.

[42] Here, it is important to distinguish the dimensions of a vector space *qua* complex space, that is, in which addition is linear under complex scalar multiplication, from dimensions of a vector space *qua* real vector space. For V and W complex vector spaces of dimension p and q respectively, $\dim_{\mathbb{C}}(V \otimes_{\mathbb{C}} W) = pq$, while $\dim_{\mathbb{R}}(V \otimes_{\mathbb{R}} W) = 4pq$.

[43] In the standard presentation, the fact that all representations of $U(1)$ are one-dimensional is a consequence of *Schur's lemma*. Namely, an irreducible unitary complex $U(1)$ representation must be 1-dimensional by Schur's lemma, since all $U(1)$ elements commute with each other and so are multiples of the identity, and each one-dimensional subspace is an invariant subspace of multiples of the identity. I find the proof in terms of tensor spaces that I mention in the main text much more transparent.

In the first two columns, the representations 3 and 2, describe the number of degrees of freedom of the particle in these spaces: vectors in $\mathbb{C}^3$ have three and in $\mathbb{C}^2$ have two. Indeed, for the same reason, we label with an '8' the representation of the gluon, whose internal components, in our geometric treatment, would be a section of $\Gamma(E^3 \otimes_T E^{*3})$, where T stands for traceless (which is necessary for parallel transport to be not only linear, but compatible with the inner product). So '8' is the number of internal degrees of freedom that such a field would have, and, its tensor structure implies it is acted on by the adjoint representation of the group action on E^3.[44]

As with the fermions, we can, of course, have different sections of vector bosons. Any such vector boson defines an affine connection D that is compatible with the fiber structure. So the structure group $G \simeq \mathrm{Aut}(E_x)$, still emerges explicitly, even "physically,"[45] by parallel transport along all the different curves, through (3.2.60).

But the gluon does not fit Table 1 because it is not a fermion, and does not decompose into a tensor product with Weyl spinors as the rest of the table does; it is a boson, and its spacetime part is a 1-form. Indeed, this is the case for all the affine connections, which, in particle physics terminology, are called the gluon, the W and the Z-bosons. These are the degrees of freedom dictating the parallel transport of color, isospin, and (hyper)charge, which, along a given spacetime curve $\gamma : [0,1] \to M$ take, respectively, the fibers of E^3, E^2, and E^1 over $\gamma(0) \in M$ to the fibers of E^3, E^2, and E^1 over $\gamma(1) \in M$, as a linear, structure-preserving transformation.

Summing up, apart from (4.3.2), we get:

$$u_R \in \Gamma(E^3 \otimes E^1_4), \quad d_R \in \Gamma(E^3 \otimes E^1_{-2}), \quad \ell_L \in \Gamma(E^2 \otimes E^1_{-3}), \quad e_R \in \Gamma(E^1_{-6}),$$

$$\tag{4.3.3}$$

and adding the vector bosons (one for each $SU(n)$), for which we include its 1-form component in spacetime:

$$\omega_n \in \Gamma(T^*M \otimes E^n \otimes_T E^{n*}), \tag{4.3.4}$$

We can conceive of each generation as having the following decomposition into five factors:

$$\mathbb{C}^{15} = (\mathbb{C}^3 \otimes \mathbb{C}^2 \otimes \mathbb{C}^1_1) \oplus (\mathbb{C}^3 \otimes \mathbb{C}^1_4) \oplus (\mathbb{C}^3 \otimes \mathbb{C}^1_{-2})$$
$$\oplus (\mathbb{C}^2 \otimes \mathbb{C}^1_{-3}) \oplus \mathbb{C}^1_{-6}. \tag{4.3.5}$$

---

[44] Here we think of the gluon as a connection on E^3, not as a Lie-algebra-valued 1-form on P. To see why I could do that, see "Relation to Connections of E Expressed without Frames of $L(E)$" section.

[45] As described in "The Structure Group G as a Holonomy Group" section, the holonomy group of isomorphic bundles $E, \bar{E}$, is identical, since each holonomy is related to by conjugation by a group element, $\mathrm{Hol}(D) = \mathrm{Hol}(\bar{D})$.

And we can finally answer the main question of this section, and indeed of the section: why do the parallel transports of different, mutually interacting particles, as sections of different vector bundles, march in step?

In the textbook tradition (see e.g. Nakahara (2003, Ch. 9)), the answer is postulated: the gauge symmetry group is not derived as preserving some physical structure, it is postulated in the definition of the principal bundle, which, as I said, is there merely auxiliary. But here I've argued that, just as tensor bundles are constructed from the underpinning geometry of *TM* and tensors have components in the spaces thus constructed, particle fields have components in internal spaces corresponding to color, isospin, and (hyper)charge, that are constructed from the underpinning geometry that is isomorphic to $\mathbb{C}^3, \mathbb{C}^2$, and $\mathbb{C}^1$, endowed with an inner product and, except in the case of $\mathbb{C}^1$, an orientation. Parallel transport marches in step because it concerns the underpinning internal geometry.

In this tensorial representation of the fields of gauge theory, there is no need for indices, except to denote the type of tensor under consideration. In the analogous spacetime case, this is called *the abstract index notation* for spacetime tensors. In that case, such tensors are invariant under passive, that is, coordinate transformations. It is only upon introducing a coordinate chart that we can talk about a spacetime tensor's components transforming under a change of coordinates. But coordinate-free, abstract spacetime tensors are *not* invariant under active diffeomorphisms, which induce a linear isomorphism between different tangent bundles.

The situation for gauge theory as I have developed it here is very similar. One can explicitly introduce internal indices by introducing a choice of frame for the vector bundle, that is, a section of the principal bundle $L(E)$. In this case, one recovers the gauge transformations via a change of frames, which amounts to a change of section of the principal bundle $L(E)$: these are construed as "passive gauge transformations." But we could also take the active, or global, point of view. Namely, given a structure-preserving linear isomorphism between vector bundles, we obtain different, but isomorphic connections. The transformation between these connections corresponds to the active view of gauge transformations (cf. Equation (3.2.57)). Nonetheless, The structure groups $SU(3) \times SU(2) \times U(1)$ are the symmetries that preserve the internal geometry, and emerge explicitly upon comparisons of parallel transported tensors via Equation (3.2.60): the holonomy group Hol(D) is invariant under linear isomorphisms and is isomorphic to the automorphism group.

4.3.2 Possible Objections

Here I will address five possible objections about the geometric viewpoint: the first is more technical, the second is conceptual; the third is metaphysical, the fourth is about completeness; and the fifth is about applications beyond the SM. All but the first two lead to concessions about my framework. Lastly, I will dissolve one apparent source of tension between this section's geometric viewpoint and Section 2's more methodological one.

First the technical possible objection: I said previously that the spinor structure of the fields comes in as a factor in a tensor product with the internal tensorial structure. But that is not exactly right for the table as I presented it: it would require me to represent the SM solely in terms of one chirality, which is certainly possible. Instead of having both right- and left-handed spinors, one can include in the table only left-handed ones; I preferred not to mix particles and anti-particles in the table, which is why I instead used both chiralities. Using a single chirality would have the advantage of being rigorous about the tensor product between internal spaces and spinors but would have the disadvantage of having to introduce complex conjugates of the representations, for example, use $\bar{3}$ instead of 3 for the first and fourth rows of Table 1, and also having to introduce q_L^c, the anti-left-handed quark doublet, and ℓ_L^c, the anti-left-handed lepton doublet. But, of course, doing this would not offend my main thesis, since complex conjugation of $\mathbb{C}^3$ is an operation that requires no more structure than I have posited; it is analogous to taking T^*M to be defined by TM (as linear functionals thereof).

Now I'll address the second, conceptual objection: given the Lagrangian of the SM written in a local coordinate system, I could extract all of the invariances and symmetry transformations directly. Invariance of the Lagrangian would constrain the internal values of the different particle fields to appropriately co-rotate. This is a true statement, but I don't think it is explanatory. For the same could, of course, be said about general covariance in general relativity. There, it is the geometric interpretation that underpins the universal coupling of all of the fields to a single spacetime geometry. But this universality could fail; for instance, if "bi-metric" Lagrangians for gravity were adopted, we could have more than one Levi-Civita connection, which could dictate parallel transport differently for different fields. Reversing the explanatory arrow, the fact that such bi-metric theories have little empirical support can be explained by the more parsimonious, familiar geometric interpretation of general relativity. Similarly, my argument here shows that the most parsimonious explanation for the current form of the Standard Model (without the analogous "bi-metrics"), is that it concerns an internal structured space, isomorphic to $\mathbb{C}^3 \times \mathbb{C}^2 \times \mathbb{C}^1$.

The third objection is very similar in spirit to the second one, but it plays out in one level lower in the hierarchy of mathematical structures. Whereas the second was about the basic geometric objects describing parallel transport, the third concerns the underpinning spaces in which the fields in question live. For the interior complex spaces I have presented are not analogous to tangent spaces with Lorentzian inner-product in all relevant senses: there is a privilege afforded to the tangent space which isn't similarly afforded to complex internal spaces, since each element of the tangent space is identified with an infinitesimal path through the base manifold: the tangent space is "soldered" onto spacetime. Thus the particular vector bundle E has to be postulated and, we must assume, shared by interacting fields.[46] Nonetheless, I maintain that the explanation afforded here distinguishes itself by putting structure, rather than symmetry, first. In contrast, the standard formalism posits both the symmetry of the principal fiber bundle and the vector bundles, and demands their compatibility, which goes unexplained.[47]

Fourthly, my description of the SM here was not complete. The attentive reader will have noticed a glaring omission: the Higgs particle is nowhere to be found in Table 1. There are, at bottom, two reasons for this omission. The first is that the Higgs would not fit in Table 1: it is a scalar field on M, not a spin 1/2 fermion, and so does not fit the required (but implicit) tensor product structure. The second, more relevant reason, is that the Higgs and spontaneous symmetry breaking (SSB) make things rather more complicated, with added *non-gauge* interactions between the Higgs and other particles through Yukawa couplings. It is mostly differences in these couplings that distinguish the three generations of the SM. The up, charm and top quarks have the same electric charge, along with the same weak and strong interactions – they primarily differ in their mass, which comes from the Higgs field. The same thing holds for the down, strange and bottom quarks, along with the electron, muon and tau leptons. And yet there is a single generation of bosons, meaning that they are all parallel transported by the same connections. The striking similarity and apparent redundancy of the three generations is one of the great mysteries of the SM, even within the

---

[46] There is a second distinction, that is due to soldering. We could still act on E with a fiber-wise linear isomorphism, with a corresponding action on the matter fields and connection-forms. This is the global, or active view of gauge transformations, on a par with the active view of smooth diffeomorphisms on a spacetime manifold. Thus, in the same way that tensors over spacetime are not invariant under active diffeomorphisms, here the gauge fields are not invariant under active linear isomorphisms. The difference between the spacetime and the gauge case is again solely due to soldering: we cannot act with a linear isomorphism over the tangent spaces without moving the spacetime points as well.

[47] See Jacobs (2021, Ch. 4.1) and references therein, for a defense of the advantages of structure-first explanations of symmetry.

standard approach. In order to address this issue in this formalism, one would need to better understand gauge-invariant construals of the Higgs mechanism and Yukawa couplings (see e.g. Struyve (2011) and Berghofer et al. (2023, Ch. 5)), in terms of invariant geometric structures along the lines that I have proposed here. I leave a full treatment of Yukawa couplings, the Higgs, and SSB for further work.

Here is the fifth possible objection, about applications beyond the SM: the interpretation of the SM that I have proposed here was very straightforward because different non-neutral charges appear only in the $\mathbb{C}^1$ sector.[48] In that one-dimensional sector, the different charges arise from tensor products (by multi-linearity) at no additional ontological price, since these products imply no additional degrees of freedom for the particles in question. So a worry might emerge that we could not account for different charges for the other forces, and that the scope of the geometric interpretation is narrower than the scope of the standard interpretation in terms of principal fiber bundles and their associated bundles.

However, at least for $SU(n)$, the geometric interpretation pursued here *can* recover all the different representations (representing different kinds of particles) by using tensor products and the internal geometric structures of the fibers $\mathbb{C}^n$ (see e.g. Coleman (1965) and Zee (2016, Ch. IV.4)). Indeed, we saw one such construction for the gauge boson, that lives in the adjoint representation, in Equation (4.3.4). That representation corresponds to a traceless tensor product between an internal space and its adjoint. And although for $n > 1$, the number of degrees of freedom of such internal tensor fields is different for different valences, this is as it should be: the number of degrees of freedom of sections of spacetime tensor fields of valence (j, k) depends on j and k, after all.

However, for some of the exceptional Lie groups, whose geometric interpretation is much more involved (cf. Adams (1996)), I believe that my interpretation might fail (e.g. if there is no minimal vector space whose structure is preserved by the group, or if there is some representation that cannot be understood in terms of tensor products of such a vector space. In these cases, my interpretation certainly becomes less natural, and so I also leave this for further study.

Finally, recall Section 2, where I gave a methodological reason for gauge symmetry: namely, that it ensured that the dynamics of fields and charges was

---

[48] In the higher dimensional $\mathbb{C}^2$ and $\mathbb{C}^3$, corresponding to $SU(2)$ and $SU(3)$, non-neutral charged matter fields of the SM appear only in the (anti-)fundamental representation, which allowed my straightforward interpretation as vectors in the internal (dual) vector space.

compatible with charge conservation. Is the new, geometric viewpoint explored in the current section in contradiction with that methodological reason? No, clearly the new viewpoint merely provides a geometrical origin to the symmetry and highlights the power of geometry in physics. Indeed, as argued in Section 2.2.2, the constraints emerging from Noether's second theorem are naturally interpreted in terms of geometric constraints on the curvature tensors and so fit nicely with this new viewpoint.

5 The Aharonov–Bohm Effect, Nonlocality, and Nonseparability

In this section I will focus on a topic that is very popular in philosophical treatments: *the Aharonov–Bohm effect*, henceforth, the AB effect. The effect is usually portrayed as being of a quantum nature; I think this is a mistake: the fact that an experimental probe of these effects employs the superposition principle is, in my view, accidental, not essential.

Instead, I will argue here that the importance of the effect is in showing there are physically salient gauge-invariant quantities that cannot be captured by the curvature tensor. The effect shows, so to speak, the fundamental significance of parallel transport, beyond what is encoded in the curvature.

Another nonessential feature of the effect as it is usually portrayed is its reliance on the nontrivial topology of space, which is a very obvious nonlocal fact. Although this portrayal is correct within the vacuum sector of the Abelian theory, even in a background space that is topologically trivial there are similar effects that have a similar significance.

Thus, in Section 5.1, I provide the standard description of the AB effect, in the vacuum sector in the Abelian theory. Next, in Section 5.2, I will show that a trivial topology does not completely close the gap between curvature and gauge invariant quantities. In the non-Abelian, vacuum case, and in a background spacetime that is topologically trivial, there still are gauge-invariant quantities that cannot be expressed using only the curvature even in a vacuum. Finally, in Section 5.3, I discuss the sense in which the content of the connection that outstrips that of the curvature is nonlocal and in which it is nonseparable. As we will see, there are important differences between the two. This section will give a very brief introduction to a third, relational reason for introducing gauge symmetry.

5.1 AB Effect in the Abelian Vacuum

Does the physical content of the gauge potential in the Abelian theory outstrip that of the Maxwell Faraday tensor? As is immediate to observe from (3.2.26), the curvature is gauge-invariant in the Abelian case. This often leads to questions about whether physical theories couldn't be entirely described without the use of the gauge *variant* potentials. But surprisingly, Abelian gauge theory has more than curvature as its fundamental degrees of freedom. The AB effect describes physical, or gauge-invariant, features of the theory that cannot be articulated using only the curvature. These features appear even in vacuum, though there they require spacetime to have (effectively) a nontrivial topology.

Historically, in order to investigate the physical significance of the gauge potential, Aharonov and Bohm proposed an electron interference experiment, in which a beam is split into two branches which go around a solenoid and are brought back together to form an interference pattern.[49] This solenoid is perfectly shielded, so that the magnetic field vanishes outside it and no electron can penetrate inside and detect the magnetic field directly.[50]

The experiment involves two different set-ups – solenoid on or off – which produce two different interference patterns. As the magnetic flux in the solenoid changes, the interference fringes shift. And yet, in both set-ups, the field-strength (i.e. the magnetic field) along the paths accessible to the charged particles is zero. So, the general outline of the experiment is: (a) the observable phenomena change when the current in the solenoid changes; and (b) the electrons that produce the phenomena are shielded from entering the region of nonzero magnetic fields; so (c) if we rule out unmediated action-at-a-distance, whatever physical difference accounts for the change must be located outside the solenoid.

Thus, to explain the different patterns, one must either conjecture a nonlocal action of the field-strength upon the particles, or regard the gauge potential as carrying ontic significance. Taking this second stance, the AB effect shows that the gauge potential cuts finer *physical* distinctions than the field-strength tensor can distinguish. How much finer?

Supposing such electrons take the paths γ_1 and γ_2 around the solenoid, we can infer from the shift in the interference pattern that there is a field-dependent contribution to the relative phase of electron paths that pass to the left and to the right of the solenoid, given by:[51]

$$e^{i\Delta} = \exp\left(i \oint_{\gamma_1 \circ \gamma_2} \mathbf{A}\right), \tag{5.1.1}$$

[49] Aharonov and Bohm's (1959) work was conducted independently of the work by Ehrenberg and Siday (1949), who proposed the same experiment with a different framing in a work that did not receive much attention at the time. According to Hiley (2013), the effect was discovered "at least three times before Aharonov and Bohm's paper"; with the first being a talk by Walter Franz, which described a similar experiment in 1939.

[50] Recently, Shech (2018) and Earman (2019) have challenged the idealizations associated with the Aharonov–Bohm effect, and Dougherty (2020) has defended them.

[51] In units for which $e/\hbar c = 1$.

where, assuming the electrostatic situation, we use bold-face to denote the spatial one-form **A** without indices. This one-form satisfies d**A** = B, where d is the spatial exterior derivative. A gauge transformation **A** → **A** + dλ will not affect (5.1.1), (for any λ ∈ $C^\infty(\Sigma)$), since $\gamma_1 \circ \gamma_2 \simeq S^1$, and so $\oint_{S^1}$ dλ = 0, by Stokes' theorem. Thus, the phase difference Δ cares only about the gauge-equivalence class of **A**.

To find out more precisely what is the physical information in the equivalence classes of the gauge potential that outstrips what can be encoded by the curvature, we proceed as follows. Given spatial gauge potentials $\mathbf{A}^1, \mathbf{A}^2$ on the spatial surface Σ, define $\mathbf{C} := \mathbf{A}^1 - \mathbf{A}^2$ where **C** is a 1-form on Σ. Suppose $\mathbf{A}^1, \mathbf{A}^2$ are such that

$$d\mathbf{A}^1 =: \mathbf{F}^1 = \mathbf{F}^2 := d\mathbf{A}^2, \tag{5.1.2}$$

and so

$$d\mathbf{C} = d\mathbf{A}^1 - d\mathbf{A}^2 = 0. \tag{5.1.3}$$

Now, if there are **C** such that **C** ≠ dλ (for any λ ∈ $C^\infty(\Sigma)$), then $\mathbf{A}^1$ and $\mathbf{A}^2$ are not related by a gauge-transformation and so are not in the same gauge-equivalence class, in spite of having the same curvature. By definition, such a **C** would be a member of $H^1(\Sigma) := \mathrm{Ker}\, d^1/\mathrm{Im}\, d^0 \subset \Lambda^1(\Sigma)$, where d^1 is the exterior derivative operator acting on the space of 1-forms on Σ, $\Lambda^1(\Sigma)$, and d^0 is that same operator acting on smooth functions (or 0-forms). This space is called the first de Rham cohomology of Σ and it is nontrivial only if there are loops in Σ that are not contractible to a point: a topological condition. For such Σ, we can therefore find distinct equivalence classes $[\mathbf{A}^1] \neq [\mathbf{A}^2]$ that can nonetheless correspond to the same electric and magnetic field. (See Belot (1998, Sec. 4) for a more thorough philosophical analysis of this paragraph's discussion.)

5.2 The Non-Abelian, Vacuum Case

In the non-Abelian case, we have an even stronger result. Namely, If two connections A and A' have the same curvature $F \neq 0$, even on a simply-connected region, and in vacuum, they are not necessarily gauge-equivalent. Therefore, generally, there is indeed more physical information captured by holonomies or Wilson loops than by the curvature. A simple example is the following: take the gauge group $SU(2)$ and base manifold $\mathbb{R}^2$. The Pauli matrices, denoted as σ_1, σ_2, and σ_3, form a basis for the Lie algebra $su(2)$:

$$\sigma_1 = \begin{bmatrix} 0 & 1 \\ 1 & 0 \end{bmatrix}, \quad \sigma_2 = \begin{bmatrix} 0 & -i \\ i & 0 \end{bmatrix}, \quad \sigma_3 = \begin{bmatrix} 1 & 0 \\ 0 & -1 \end{bmatrix}.$$

The Pauli matrices satisfy the following algebraic relations, known as the Pauli algebra:

$$\sigma_1^2 = \sigma_2^2 = \sigma_3^2 = \text{Id} \quad \text{(where Id is the identity matrix)}$$

$$\sigma_i\sigma_j = -\sigma_j\sigma_i \quad \text{for } i \neq j \quad \text{(antisymmetry)} \tag{5.2.1}$$

$$\sigma_i\sigma_j = \delta_{ij}\text{Id} + i\epsilon_{ijk}\sigma_k \quad \text{(where } \epsilon_{ijk} \text{ is the Levi-Civita symbol)}$$

Now consider

$$A = -iy\sigma_3 dx + ix\sigma_3 dy \tag{5.2.2}$$

$$A' = i\sigma_1 dx - i\sigma_2 dy \tag{5.2.3}$$

In both cases, the term $dA = dA' = 0$, and using (5.2.2) it is simple to verify that, calculating the curvatures $V = dA + A \wedge A$ we get:

$$F = F' = 2i\sigma_3 dx \wedge dy. \tag{5.2.4}$$

If A and A' were gauge-related, there should exist $g \in C^\infty(\mathbb{R}^2, SU(2))$ such that $A' = gAg^{-1} - dg\, g^{-1}$, in which case $F' = gFg^{-1} = F$. That is, F should be invariant under such a g, or, infinitesimally, V should commute with the generator of the transformation. Since $F \propto \sigma_3$, and, from (5.2.1), the only transformations that commute with σ_3 are generated by σ_3, we would have $g_o = e^{i\theta\sigma_3}$ for some $\theta(x,y)$. From (5.2.2), since A only contains σ_3, we get that $g_o A g_o^{-1} = A$ and thus

$$g_o A g_o^{-1} - dg_o\, g_o^{-1} = A - id\theta\sigma_3. \tag{5.2.5}$$

Clearly, since this expression still only contains σ_3, there is no θ that can transform it into A'.

5.3 Nonlocality and Nonseparability

It is often said (cf. e.g. Belot (1998), Healey (2007), Healey & Gomes (2021), Myrvold (2011)) that the Aharonov–Bohm effect of classical electromagnetism evinces a form of nonlocality, something that otherwise might have been thought of as confined to nonclassical physics. In the same vein, it is often said that gauge-invariant quantities are nonlocal. In Section 5.3.1 I will argue that the nonlocality in question is relatively benign. This argument will lead us to yet another reason for gauge symmetry, introduced by Rovelli (2014). In Section 5.3.2 I will argue that, notwithstanding Section's 5.3.1 deflationary account of nonlocality, there is still an interesting notion of nonseparability at play in gauge theories, but such a notion is the norm in physical theories, not the exception. Finally, in Section 5.4, I conclude this section and this Element.

5.3.1 Nonlocality and Rovelli's Relational Reason for Gauge

In Equation (5.1.1), the AB effect was quantified by *the holonomy* of the connection along a closed curve (which we first encountered in Section 4.2, cf. Equation (3.2.60), and will discuss further in Section 5.3.2; cf. Equation (5.3.1)). This is a nonlocal, gauge-invariant quantity, and it raises the question of whether all gauge-invariant quantities are in some sense nonlocal. And this question has a long and vexed history, which I will not be able to fully cover here (cf. Berghofer et al. (2023); Carrozza & Höohn (2022); Earman (1987) and Gomes (2024b, Sec. 3.4)). All I can offer is a summary.

Of course, there are gauge-invariant quantities that are local. These are easy to find using the matter fields, $\psi\overline{\psi}$ is just one example. But even in vacuum they are easy to find: $F_I^{\mu\nu}F_{\mu\nu}^I$ is gauge-invariant.[52] But, as we saw in the previous section, not all gauge-invariant quantities could be written in terms of the curvature. A certain set of variables can be used to describe all the physical states of a system iff they can describe all the possible initial data for that system, so it pays to have a small digression into the canonical formalism.

As we saw in Section 2, the equations of motion of theories such as general relativity and Yang-Mills are not all independent, and thus they only uniquely determine the evolution of a subset of the original degrees of freedom. In practice, this means that initial data for these two theories must satisfy elliptic differential equations. Since elliptic equations do not describe anything propagating – their boundary conditions are instantaneous and nonlocally determine the solution within the bounded region – we get a nonlocal parametrization of initial data that satisfy these constraints.

There is thus a certain freedom in choosing which "components of the fields" will be uniquely propagated, or will evolve deterministically; each choice corresponds to a gauge-fixing, or, equivalently, to a parametrization of the solutions of the initial value constraints. In other words, each gauge-fixing can be seen as a choice of conjugate degrees of freedom – configuration and conjugate momentum variables – that are uniquely propagated because they satisfy the constraints and are freely specifiable; cf. Gomes and Butterfield (2022) for more about this interpretation of the initial value constraints and nonlocality.

So that is a way of seeing nonlocality of gauge-invariant quantities through the lens of the canonical (or Hamiltonian) approach to these theories. From the covariant perspective we can give another heuristic explanation. The connection-form determines parallel transport on a vector bundle E, but it is

---

[52] Similarly, with general relativity, we could find gauge-invariant quantities that have support over a single point: for example, the value of any curvature scalar on a point determined by the value of a complete set of Kretschmann-Komar scalars: see Gomes (2024b, Sec. 4.3).

not invariant: it will transform if we apply a fiber-preserving linear automorphism on E. Intuitively, in order to extract invariant information from parallel transport, we must somehow compare parallel transported objects. And this is a nonlocal operation. Heuristically, we could see this from the inhomogeneous, that is, nontensorial transformation properties of the connection, given in Equation (3.2.11) (for the Ehresmann connection, or (3.2.44) for the projection onto a section). Namely, in order to extract the content of the connection that is invariant under gauge transformations we need to eliminate this derivative; that is, we need to use integration.

Another way to describe gauge-invariant quantities is to anchor the representation of a state to a physical system, with the ensuing representation being straightforwardly understood in terms of gauge-invariant relations to this physical system (see Carrozza & Höhn (2022); Gomes (2024b) for a defense of this view). For instance, given a set of four scalar fields obeying functionally independent Klein-Gordon equations, we can understand harmonic gauge in general relativity as using these fields as coordinates on a region of spacetime (cf. Bamonti (2023) and references therein). Similarly, in gauge theory, a nowhere vanishing charged matter field could select an internal frame for a vector bundle, and we would describe other fields relative to this frame. In electromagnetism, unitary gauge can be understood in this way, and it is completely local (see e.g. Gomes (2024b, Sec. 4.2) and Wallace (2024)).[53] But, again, one cannot pick out a frame using only local properties of parallel transport: it is for this reason that gauge-fixings based only on the connection – such as Coulomb gauge – are nonlocal: in order to describe this particular kind of internal frame, we need to resort to properties of the field at spatially separated points.

Thus we arrive at the doorstep of another answer to the question of "why gauge," introduced by Rovelli (2014). Namely, that gauge freedom is essentially relational in character. This is easy to motivate within the geometric perspective I have developed here, for example, a vector in a vector space *is not* invariant under rotations, but the inner product between two vectors, a relational quantity, *is*. And similarly with internal quantities: for instance, the decomposition of a quark field into three colors is gauge-dependent, but measured and coupled to some other physical system these components can be interpreted invariantly.

Indeed, Rovelli argues more broadly, that symmetry-invariant descriptions of most physical systems arise only via relations between different parts of those systems. And, since it is an answer that this Element is too short to do justice to, I defer to Rovelli's (2014, p. 7) excellent summary:

---

[53] But there is nothing analogous to such frames for general non-Abelian groups.

Gauge invariance is not just mathematical redundancy; it is an indication of the relational character of fundamental observables in physics. These do not refer to properties of a single entity. They refer to relational properties between entities: relative velocity, relative localization, *relative orientation in internal space*, and so on.[...] Gauge is ubiquitous. It is not unphysical redundancy of our mathematics. It reveals the relational structure of our world. [my italics]

This relational understanding of gauge fits nicely with the geometrical viewpoint provided in Section 4.

In sum, nonlocality arises because the function that takes the original local degrees of freedom in an arbitrary frame to a unique frame that is defined "physically" or via properties of the fields, is often nonlocal: the value of an element in the subset at point x depends on the values of the original degrees of freedom at other points (see Gomes & Butterfield (2022, Sec. 1.1, point (3)) for more discussion about this sort of (nonsignaling) classical nonlocality).[54] And that is just because we determine, or "construct" the frame from properties of the fields, and some invariant relations between different components of some of the fields are nonlocal.

Gomes (2019, 2021) and Gomes & Riello (2021) develop Rovelli's ideas further, distinguishing two aspects of the 'coupling' of systems that are related to symmetries. The first aspect is closer to Rovelli's (2014) justification for gauge, briefly described previously. As they put it: in order to join gauge-invariant descriptions of subsystems, we need to employ gauge degrees of freedom. The second aspect of coupling that is related to symmetries is that there is more than one way to successfully couple gauge-invariant subsystems, and this multiplicity gives rise to a symmetry with empirical significance. This second notion is tightly related to that of nonseparability of physical systems, which we now turn to.

5.3.2 Nonseparability

As I said, the notion of nonlocality that I described earlier applies more generally than what is required for the AB effect: most gauge-fixings lead to such a nonlocal representation of the state (cf. Gomes (2024b, Sec. 3)). But as we will see in this section, the AB effect also illustrates another, related idea: *nonseparability*. Broadly, the idea is that gauge-invariant states on patches or regions of space or spacetime do not uniquely determine the gauge-invariant state on the union of those patches or regions. In Gomes (2021), I also argued

---

[54] It is clear that relativistic causality holds for the isomorphism-invariant facts, since (quasi-) hyperbolicity of the equations of motion ensures causality is respected for one choice of metric or gauge potential representing the isomorphism-equivalence class (e.g. Lorenz or DeDonder gauge for electromagnetism and general relativity, respectively).

that this kind of nonseparability, or holism, can be construed as an empirical manifestation of symmetries as applied 'externally' to a subsystem. In other words, there are often many ways in which to put together the physical states of two patches or regions into a whole, and all these different ways are related to each other by a symmetry transformation that acts only on one of the subsystems. Apart from the case of electromagnetism, the existence of such transformations is contingent on special – specially homogeneous – states at the boundary of the region.[55]

Similar versions of separability are offered by Healey (2007, p. 26), who calls it *Spatial Separability*, Belot (1998, p. 540), whose term is *Synchronic Locality*, and Myrvold (2011, p. 427), who calls it *Patchy Separability*. The guiding idea there is very similar to the one I described earlier (from Gomes (2021)): it is that the state of a region supervenes on assignments of intrinsic properties to patches of the region, where the patches may be taken to be arbitrarily small.

But, whereas Gomes (2021) formulates these properties using gauge-fixings of the states and considers also the non-Abelian theory, each of these papers formulates the question of separability for electromagnetism in holonomy variables. Although their formulation is inadequate to deal with non-Abelian theories – and so Gomes (2021) is more general – for the vacuum Abelian case the use of holonomies is simpler and adequate. So in this section, I will describe nonseparability in electromagnetism using holonomies.

Given the space of loops – smooth embeddings into spacetime $c : S^1 \rightarrow M$ – one can form a basis of gauge-invariant quantities, called *holonomies*:

$$H(c) := \exp \oint_c A. \qquad (5.3.1)$$

Clearly these are gauge-invariant, since under a gauge transformation

$$H(c) \mapsto H(c) \exp \oint_c (d\lambda) = H(c) \exp ((\lambda(\bar{x}) - \lambda(\bar{x}))) = H(c), \qquad (5.3.2)$$

where $\bar{x}$ is taken as any base point for the loop c.

---

[55] As also shown by Greaves & Wallace (2014) and Wallace (2022), the external symmetries that acquire empirical significance in this way must act trivially on the boundary of the region in question but nontrivially on the regional state on the bulk, away from the boundary. The major difference between these two papers and Gomes (2021) is that the latter uses a gauge-fixed formulation that applies individually to any choice of subsystem states, whereas Greaves & Wallace (2014) and Wallace (2022) focus on isolated subsystems, and apply to entire sectors of theories. See Gomes & Riello (2021, Sec. 6) for a mathematical formula, valid also in the non-Abelian theory, that describes the degeneracy of global physical states that results from gluing the same subsystem physical states.

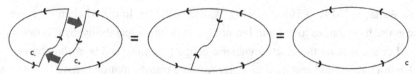

Figure 3 The composition properties of holonomies guarantee separability in the absence of holes: the two arrows going along the middle line cancel out.

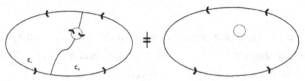

Figure 4 In the presence of holes, there may be holonomies that are not separable into holonomies that are intrinsic to the patches that do not contain the holes.

In order to compose holonomies for different curves, we take c_- an open curve that ends where c_+, another open curve, begins. Then we define the composition $c_- \circ c_+$ as a map from $[-1/2, 1/2]$ into M, which takes $[-1/2, 0]$ to traverse c_- and $[0, 1/2]$ to traverse c_+. Following this composition law, it is easy to see that

$$H(c_- \circ c_+) = H(c_-)H(c_+) \tag{5.3.3}$$

with the right-hand side understood as complex multiplication in the Abelian case. Thus, if $c_- = c_+^{-1}$ (opposite orientations), $H(c_-)H(c_+) = \text{Id}$. This property underlies the graphical calculus of Figure 3.

Suppose we split a simply connected region into two patches that only overlap in their common, simply-connected boundary. By composing regional loops c_+, c_- going in opposite directions at the boundary, since the opposite contributions of those segments cancel out, it is true, as Myrvold (2011) argues, that we recover the gauge-invariant holonomy corresponding to a larger loop c not contained in either region. In this case, as seen in Figure 3, any holonomy can be recovered by the holonomy of curves intrinsic to the patches and so Abelian gauge theory in vacuum is separable.

According to Myrvold (2011), separability fails only for nonsimply connected manifolds. For, as can be seen in Figure 4, holonomies intrinsic to the two regions could not cancel out around the hole, for they are not collinear there.

But Myrvold (2011) considers only the vacuum case. And, as becomes evident using gauge-fixings (cf. Gomes (2021)), in the presence of charges we can get nonseparability even in a trivial topological background (see also Greaves

& Wallace (2014); 't Hooft (1980); Wallace (2022)). In the Abelian case, we can use holonomies to exhibit, but not quantify, this separability, as follows.

Let again A be the electromagnetic gauge potential, and $\psi, \overline{\psi}$ the charged Klein-Gordon field and its conjugate. A gauge transformation maps

$$A(x) \mapsto A(x) + d\lambda(x), \quad \psi(x) \mapsto \exp(i\lambda(x))\psi(x), \quad \overline{\psi}(x) \mapsto \exp -(i\lambda(x))\overline{\psi}(x).$$
$$\text{(5.3.4)}$$

Given one positive and one negative charge at the points x_1 and x_2 (fields that have a singular support on x_1 and x_2): ψ and $\overline{\psi}$, and an open curve c whose initial and final points are x_1 and x_2, respectively, then:

$$Q(c) := \overline{\psi} \exp\left(i \int_c A\right) \psi \qquad \text{(5.3.5)}$$

is also gauge-invariant, since

$$\exp\left(i \int_c A\right) \mapsto \exp\left(i(\lambda(x_1) - \lambda(x_2)) + i \int_c A\right)$$
$$= \exp(i\lambda(x_1)) \exp\left(i \int_c A\right) \exp(-i\lambda(x_2)), \qquad \text{(5.3.6)}$$

which cancels with the transformations of ψ and $\overline{\psi}$, by (5.3.4). Here, because we are assuming there are no charges except at the ends of c, we cannot break $Q(c)$ up into gauge-invariant quantities $Q(c_{1,2,\dots})$ attached to smaller segments $c_{1,2,\dots} \subset c$.[56]

5.4 Conclusion

Here is one thing the AB effect illustrates: even though curvature encodes the local geometric tensors that involve derivatives of the connection, there are geometric facts that arise from the comparison of parallel transported vectors along different curves: they do not involve derivatives of the connection, but their integrals. This applies to internal as well as spacetime vectors: there are several treatments of (close analogues of) the AB effect within general relativity; cf. Anandan (1977), Dowker (1967), Ford & Vilenkin (1981). And although topological facts are, in a sense, nonlocal, these facts are mostly important in

---

[56] We would get, for example, for c' a segment between x'_1 and x'_2:

$$Q(c') \mapsto e^{i(\lambda(x_2) - \lambda(x'_2))} Q(c') e^{-i(\lambda(x_1) - \lambda(x'_1))} \neq Q(c'), \qquad \text{(5.3.7)}$$

If we had a plenum of the charged field, that is, $\psi(x) \neq 0$, $\forall x \in \Sigma$, we could indeed find a basis of local gauge-invariant functions, equivalent to unitary gauge; this is what allows Wallace's (2014) separable treatment of the AB effect.

the Abelian case, where they merely allow sufficiently distinct connections all with the same curvature.

While it is true that holonomies in electromagnetism are nonlocal symmetry invariant quantities, the kind of nonlocality that they evince is general. For instance, it arises from using properties of the fields to fix the internal frames in which initial data is uniquely propagated by the equations of motion, a procedure called *gauge-fixing*.

But that is not the most important point that is illustrated by the AB effect. As we saw, the effect also illustrates nonseparability (even in the vacuum, Abelian case). Nonseparability is a feature not only of gauge theories, but also of other theories with symmetry, even nonrelativistic particle mechanics. It implies that fixing the symmetry-invariant content of subsystems does not fix the symmetry-invariant content of the composition of those subsystems. In other words: the physical content intrinsic to subsystems can be put together in more ways than one. Since these different ways are obtained from each other by "external symmetry transformations" (cf. Gomes (2021)), we see here a new reason for introducing at least some symmetries: because they describe the physically inequivalent ways to couple the same subsystem states.

References

Adams, J. F. (1996). *Lectures on Exceptional Lie Groups*. Chicago, IL: University of Chicago Press.

Aharonov, Y., & Bohm, D. (1959). Significance of electromagnetic potentials in the quantum theory. *The Physical Review*, *115*, 485–491. https://link.aps.org/doi/10.1103/PhysRev.115.485.

Anandan, J. (1977). Gravitational and rotational effects in quantum interference. *Physical Review D*, *15*, 1448–1457. https://link.aps.org/doi/10.1103/PhysRevD.15.1448.

Atiyah, M. (1957). Complex analytic connections in fibre bundles. *Transactions of the American Mathematical Society 85*(1), 181–207.

Avery, S. G., & Schwab, B. U. W. (2016). Noether's second theorem and ward identities for gauge symmetries. *Journal of High Energy Physics*, *2016*(2). http://dx.doi.org/10.1007/JHEP02(2016)031.

Baez, J., & Munian, J. (1994). *Gauge Fields, Knots and Gravity*. Singapore: World Scientific.

Bamonti, N. (2023). *What is a Reference Frame in General Relativity?* https://arxiv.org/abs/2307.09338.

Belot, G. (1998). Understanding electromagnetism. *The British Journal for the Philosophy of Science*, *49*(4), 531–555. https://doi.org/10.1093/bjps/49.4.531.

Berghofer, P., Francois, J., Friederich, S., et al. (2023). *Elements in the Foundations of Physics: Gauge Symmetries, Symmetry Breaking, and Gauge-Invariant Approaches*. Cambridge, UK Cambridge University Press.

Bonora, L., & Cotta-Ramusino, P. (1983). Some remarks on BRS transformations, anomalies and the cohomology of the Lie algebra of the group of gauge transformations. *Communications in Mathematical Physics*, *87*(4), 589–603. http://link.springer.com/10.1007/BF01208267.

Boothby, W. M. (2010). *An introduction to differentiable manifolds and Riemannian geometry* (Rev. 2. ed., [Nachdr.] ed.). Amsterdam: Academic Press. (Literaturverz. S. 403–409)

Brading, K., & Brown, H. R. (2000). *Noether's theorems and gauge symmetries* hep-th/0009058.

Brading, K., & Brown, H. R. (2003). Symmetries and Noether's theorems. In K. Brading & E. Castellani (Eds.), *Symmetries in Physics: Philosophical Reflections* (pp. 89–109). Cambridge: Cambridge University Press. https://doi.org/10.1017/CBO9780511535369.006.

Brown, H. (1999). Aspects of objectivity in quantum mechanics. In J. Butterfield & C. Pagonis (Eds.), *From Physics to Philosophy*. Cambridge: Cambridge University Press. http://philsci-archive.pitt.edu/223/.

Brown, H. (2022). Do symmetries 'explain' conservation laws? The modern converse Noether theorem vs pragmatism. In J. Read & N. J. Teh (Eds.), *The Philosophy and Physics of Noether's Theorems: A Centenary Volume* (pp. 144–168). Cambridge: Cambridge University Press. https://doi.org/10.1017/9781108665445.008.

Carrozza, S., & Höhn, P. A. (2022). Edge modes as reference frames and boundary actions from post-selection. *Journal of High Energy Physics*, *2022*(2). https://doi.org/10.1007/jhep02(2022)172.

Ciambelli, L., & Leigh, R. G. (2021). *Lie Algebroids and the Geometry of Off-Shell BRST*. *Nuclear Physics B*, 972, 115553, https://doi.org/10.1016/j.nuclphysb.2021.115553.

Coleman, S. (1965). Fun with SU(3). In *Seminar on High-Energy Physics and Elementary Particles* (pp. 331–352). Boston, MA: MIT press.

de León, M., & Zajac, M. (2020). Hamilton–Jacobi theory for gauge field theories. *Journal of Geometry and Physics*, *152*, 103636. http://dx.doi.org/10.1016/j.geomphys.2020.103636.

Dougherty, J. (2020). The non-ideal theory of the Aharonov–Bohm effect. *Synthese*, *198*(2021), 12195–12221.

Dowker, J. S. (1967). A gravitational Aharonov–Bohm effect. *Il Nuovo Cimento B (1965–1970)*, *52*, 129–135.

Earman, J. (1987). Locality, nonlocality and action at a distance: A skeptical review of some philosophical dogmas. In R. Kargon, P. Achinstein, & W. T. Kelvin (Eds.), *Kelvin's Baltimore Lectures and Modern Theoretical Physics: Historical and Philosophical Perspectives* (pp. 449–490). Cambridge, MA: MIT Press. http://d-scholarship.pitt.edu/12972/.

Earman, J. (2002). Gauge matters. *Philosophy of Science*, *69*(S3), S209–S220. https://doi.org/10.1086/341847.

Earman, J. (2003). Tracking down gauge: An ode to the constrained Hamiltonian formalism. In K. Brading & E. Castellani (Eds.), *Symmetries in Physics: Philosophical Reflections* (pp. 140–162). Cambridge: Cambridge University Press.

Earman, J. (2004). Curie's principle and spontaneous symmetry breaking. *International Studies in the Philosophy of Science*, *18*(2 & 3), 173–198. https://doi.org/10.1080/0269859042000311299.

Earman, J. (2019). The role of idealizations in the Aharonov–Bohm effect. *Synthese*, *196*(5), 1991–2019. https://doi.org/10.1007/s11229-017-1522-9.

Ehrenberg, W., & Siday, R. E. (1949). The refractive index in electron optics and the principles of dynamics. *Proceedings of the Physical Society. Section B, 62*(1), 8–21. https://doi.org/10.1088/0370-1301/62/1/303.

Fischer, A. E., & Marsden, J. E. (1979). The initial value problem and the dynamical formulation of general relativity. In S. W. Hawking (Ed.), *General Relativity: An Einstein Centenary Survey*. New York: cambridge university press, pp. 138–211.

Ehresmann, Charles. 1950. Les connexions infinitésimales dans un espace fibré différentiable. Séminaire Bourbaki : années 1948/49 – 1949/50 – 1950/51, exposés 1-49, Séminaire Bourbaki, no. 1 (1952), Talk no. 24, 16 p.

Ford, L. H., & Vilenkin, A. (1981). A gravitational analogue of the Aharonov–Bohm effect. *Journal of Physics A: Mathematical and General, 14*(9), 2353–2357. https://doi.org/10.1088/0305-4470/14/9/030.

Göckeler, M., & Schücker, T. (1989). *Differential Geometry, Gauge Theories, and Gravity*. Cambridge: Cambridge University Press.

Gomes, H. (2019). Gauging the boundary in field-space. *Studies in History and Philosophy of Science Part B: Studies in History and Philosophy of Modern Physics*. www.sciencedirect.com/science/article/pii/S1355219818302144. https://doi.org/10.1016/j.shpsb.2019.04.002.

Gomes, H. (2021). Holism as the significance of gauge symmetries. *European Journal of Philosophy of Science, 11*, 87.

Gomes, H. (2022). Noether charges, gauge-invariance, and non-separability. In J. Read, and N. J. Teh, (Eds.), *The Philosophy and Physics of Noether's Theorems: A Centenary Volume* (pp. 296–321). Cambridge: Cambridge University Press. https://doi.org/10.1017/9781108665445.013.

Gomes, H. (2024a). Gauge theory as the geometry of internal vector spaces. https://philsci-archive.pitt.edu/id/eprint/24069.

Gomes, H. (2024b). Representational schemes for theories with symmetries. https://philsci-archive.pitt.edu/id/eprint/24070.

Gomes, H., & Butterfield, J. (2022). How to choose a gauge? The case of Hamiltonian electromagnetism. *Erkenntnis. 89*, 1581–1615. https://doi.org/10.1007/s10670-022-00597-9.

Gomes, H., Hopfmüller, F., & Riello, A. (2019). A unified geometric framework for boundary charges and dressings: Non-abelian theory and matter. *Nuclear Physics B, 941*, 249–315. www.sciencedirect.com/science/article/pii/S0550321319300483. https://doi.org/10.1016/j.nuclphysb.2019.02.020.

Gomes, H., & Riello, A. (2017). The observer's ghost: Notes on a field space connection. *Journal of High Energy Physics (JHEP), 05*, 017. https://link.springer.com/article/10.10072FJHEP0528201729017. article number 17.

Gomes, H., & Riello, A. (2021). The quasilocal degrees of freedom of Yang-Mills theory. *SciPost Physics, 10*, 130. https://scipost.org/10.21468/SciPostPhys.10.6.130.

Greaves, H., & Wallace, D. (2014). Empirical consequences of symmetries. *British Journal for the Philosophy of Science, 65*(1), 59–89.

Guillemin, V., & Pollack, A. (2010). *Differential Topology*. London: AMS Chelsea. https://books.google.co.uk/books?id=FdRhAQAAQBAJ.

Healey, R. (2007). *Gauging What's Real: The Conceptual Foundations of Gauge Theories*. Oxford: Oxford University Press.

Healey, R., & Gomes, H. (2021). Holism and nonseparability in physics. In E. N. Zalta (Ed.), *The Stanford Encyclopedia of Philosophy* (Spring 2016 ed.). Stanford: Metaphysics Research Lab, Stanford University. https://plato.stanford.edu/archives/spr2016/entries/physics-holism/.

Henneaux, M., & Teitelboim, C. (1992). *Quantization of Gauge Systems*. Princeton: Princeton University Press.

Hiley, B. (2013). The early history of the Aharonov–Bohm effect. *arXiv preprint arXiv:1304.4736.*

Jacobs, C. (2021). *Symmetries as a Guide to theStructure of Physical Quantities* (Unpublished doctoral dissertation). University of Oxford.

Jacobs, C. (2023). The metaphysics of fibre bundles. *Studies in History and Philosophy of Science, 97*, 34–43. www.sciencedirect.com/science/article/pii/S0039368122001777. https://doi.org/10.1016/j.shpsa.2022.11.010.

Kobayaschi, S. (1957). Theory of connections. *Annali di Matematica 43*, 119–194. https://doi.org/10.1007/BF02411907.

Kobayashi, S., & Nomizu, K. (1963). *Foundations of Differential Geometry. Vol I*. New York: Interscience, a division of John Wiley.

Kolar, I., Michor, P., & Slovak, J. (1993). *Natural Operations in Differential Geometry*. Berlin: Springer.

Kosmann-Schwarzbach, Y. (2011). *The Noether Theorems: Invariance and Conservation Laws in the Twentieth Century*. New York: Springer Science+Business Media. (Translated by Bertram E. Schwarzbach)

Lovelock, D. (1972). The four-dimensionality of space and the Einstein tensor. *Journal of Mathematical Physics, 13*, 874–876. https://doi.org/10.1063/1.1666069.

Mackenzie, K. C. H. (2005). *General Theory of Lie Groupoids and Lie Algebroids*. Cambridge University Press. https://doi.org/10.1017/CBO9781107325883.

Martin, C. A. (2002). Gauge principles, gauge arguments and the logic of nature. *Philosophy of Science, 69*(S3), S221–S234.

Michor, P. W. (2008). *Topics in Differential Geometry* (No. volume 93). Providence, RI: American Mathematical Society. (Includes bibliographical references (pages 479–488) and index. Description based on print version record.)

Myrvold, W. C. (2011). Nonseparability, classical, and quantum. *The British Journal for the Philosophy of Science, 62*(2), 417–432. https://doi.org/10.1093/bjps/axq036.

Nakahara, M. (2003). *Geometry, Topology and Physics*. Bristol: Institute of Physics.

Noether, E. (1918). Invariante variationsprobleme. *Nachr. D. König. Gesellsch. D. Wiss. Zu Göttingen, Math-phys. Klasse, 7*, 235–257. English translation by M. A. Tavel: https://arxiv.org/abs/physics/0503066.

Olver, P. (1986). *Applications of Lie Groups to Differential Equations*. New York: Springer-Verlag.

O'Raifertaigh, L. (1997). *The Dawning of Gauge Theory*. Princeton: Princeton University Press. www.jstor.org/stable/j.ctv10vm2qt.

Rosenstock, S., & Weatherall, J. O. (2016). A categorical equivalence between generalized holonomy maps on a connected manifold and principal connections on bundles over that manifold. *Journal of Mathematical Physics, 57*(10), 102902. http://philsci-archive.pitt.edu/11904/.

Rosenstock, S., & Weatherall, J. O. (2018). Erratum: "A categorical equivalence between generalized holonomy maps on a connected manifold and principal connections on bundles over that manifold". *Journal of Mathematical Physics, 59*(2), 029901.

Rovelli, C. (2014). Why gauge? *Foundation of Physics, 44*(1), 91–104. https://doi.org/10.1007/s10701-013-9768-7.

Ryder, L. H. (1996). *Quantum Field Theory*. Cambridge: Cambridge University Press.

Sardanashvily, G. (2009). *Fibre Bundles, Jet Manifolds and Lagrangian Theory: Lectures for Theoreticians*. arXiv:0908.1886.

Schutz, B. F. (1980). *Geometric Methods of Mathematical Physics*. Cambridge: Cambridge University Press.

Shech, E. (2018). Idealizations, essential self-adjointness, and minimal model explanation in the Aharonov–Bohm effect. *Synthese, 195*(11), 4839–4863. https://doi.org/10.1007/s11229-017-1428-6.

Steenrod, N. 1951. *The Topology of Fibre Bundles*. Series: Princeton Mathematical Series. Princeton Landmarks in Mathematics and Physics. Princeton University Press.

Struyve, W. (2011). Gauge invariant accounts of the Higgs mechanism. *Studies in History and Philosophy of Science Part B: Studies* in History and Philosophy of Modern Physics, *42*(4), 226–236. www.sciencedirect.com/science/article/pii/S1355219811000384. https://doi.org/10.1016/j.shpsb.2011.06.003.

Swanson, N. (2019). On the ostrogradski instability, or, why physics really uses second derivatives. *The British Journal for the Philosophy of Science.* http://philsci-archive.pitt.edu/15932/.

Teller, P. (1997). A metaphysics for contemporary field theories. *Studies in History and Philosophy of Modern Physics, 28*(4), 507–522.

Teller, P. (2000). The gauge argument. *Philosophy of Science, 67*, S466–S481. www.jstor.org/stable/188688.

Thierry-Mieg, J. (1980). Geometrical reinterpretation of faddeev-popov ghost particles and brs transformations. *Journal of Mathematical Physics, 21*(12), 2834–2838. https://doi.org/10.1063/1.524385.

't Hooft, G. (1980). Gauge theories and the forces between elementary particles. *Scientific American, 242*, 90–166.

Wallace, D. (2009). *QFT, Antimatter and Symmetry.* Unpublished Manuscript, http://arxiv.org/abs/0903.3018.

Wallace, D. (2014). Deflating the Aharonov-Bohm effect. *arxiv: 1407.5073.*

Wallace, D. (2022). Isolated systems and their symmetries, part II: Local and global symmetries of field theories. *Studies in History and Philosophy of Science, 92*, 249–259. www.sciencedirect.com/science/article/pii/S0039368122000267. https://doi.org/10.1016/j.shpsa.2022.01.016.

Wallace, D. (2024). *Gauge Invariance through Gauge Fixing. Studies in History and Philosophy of Science, 108*, 38–45.

Weatherall, J. (2016). Fiber bundles, Yang–Mills theory, and general relativity. *Synthese, 193*(8), 2389–2425. http://philsci-archive.pitt.edu/11481/.

Wells, R. O. N. (1988). *The Mathematical Heritage of Hermann Weyl.* New York: American Mathematical Society. https://books.google.co.uk/books?id=e0MECAAAQBAJ.

Weyl, H. (1929). Gravitation and the electron. *Proceedings of the National Academy of Sciences of the United States of America, 15*(4), 323–334. www.ncbi.nlm.nih.gov/pmc/articles/PMC522457/.

Wu, T. T., & Yang, C. N. (1975). Concept of nonintegrable phase factors and global formulation of gauge fields. *Physical Review D, 12*, 3845–3857. https://link.aps.org/doi/10.1103/PhysRevD.12.3845.

Yang, C. N. (1983). Articles. In *Selected papers (1945–1980) of chen ning yang* (pp. 101–567). W. H. Freeman. www.worldscientific.com/doi/abs/10.1142/9789812703354_0002. https://doi.org/10.1142/9789812703354_0002.

Yang, C. N., & Mills, R. L. (1954). Conservation of isotopic spin and isotopic gauge invariance. *Physical Review*, *96*, 191–195. https://link.aps.org/doi/10.1103/PhysRev.96.191.

Zee, A. (2016). *Group Theory in a Nutshell for Physicists*. Princeton: Princeton University Press. (Literaturverzeichnis: Seite 581–582. - Hier auch später erschienene, unveränderte Nachdrucke).

Cambridge Elements ≡

The Philosophy of Physics

James Owen Weatherall
University of California, Irvine

James Owen Weatherall is Professor of Logic and Philosophy of Science at the University of California, Irvine. He is the author, with Cailin O'Connor, of *The Misinformation Age: How False Beliefs Spread* (Yale, 2019), which was selected as a *New York Times* Editors' Choice and Recommended Reading by *Scientific American*. His previous books were *Void: The Strange Physics of Nothing* (Yale, 2016) and the *New York Times* bestseller *The Physics of Wall Street: A Brief History of Predicting the Unpredictable* (Houghton Mifflin Harcourt, 2013). He has published approximately fifty peer-reviewed research articles in journals in leading physics and philosophy of science journals and has delivered over 100 invited academic talks and public lectures.

About the Series

This Cambridge Elements series provides concise and structured introductions to all the central topics in the philosophy of physics. The Elements in the series are written by distinguished senior scholars and bright junior scholars with relevant expertise, producing balanced, comprehensive coverage of multiple perspectives in the philosophy of physics.

Cambridge Elements ≡

The Philosophy of Physics

Printed in the United States
by Baker & Taylor Publisher Services